Walks in the Kent Hills

Twenty country walks around the Kent Hills

JANET SPAYNE
and
AUDREY KRYNSKI

*Countryside Books' walking guides cover
most areas of England and Wales.*

*To view our complete range of books
please visit us at*
www.countrysidebooks.co.uk

Walks in the Kent Hills

Twenty country walks
around the Kent Hills

JANET SPAYNE
and
AUDREY KRYNSKI

COUNTRYSIDE BOOKS
NEWBURY, BERKSHIRE

First published 1976

Fourth edition, fully revised and updated, published 2000

© Janet Spayne and Audrey Krynski 2000

COUNTRYSIDE BOOKS
3 Catherine Road
Newbury, Berkshire

Publisher's Note
At the time of publication all footpaths used in these walks were
designated as official footpaths or rights of way, but it should be
borne in mind that diversion orders may be made from time to
time. Although every care has been taken in the preparation of this
guide, neither the author nor the publisher can accept
responsibility for those who stray from the rights of way.

ISBN 1 85306 631 1

Designed by Graham Whiteman

Maps by King and King
Cover photograph of Crockham Hill
by David Sellman

Produced through MRM Associates Ltd., Reading
Printed by J. W. Arrowsmith Ltd., Bristol

AREA MAP SHOWING LOCATION OF THE WALKS

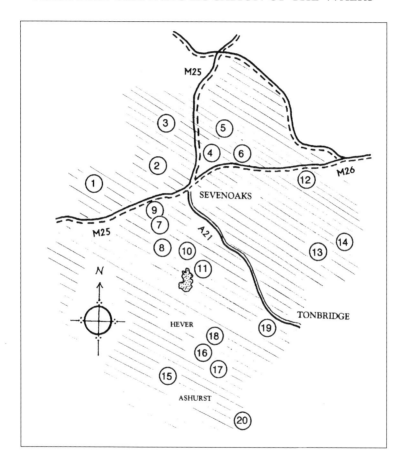

Contents

Introduction

Compiling this book of walks has been an enjoyable task chiefly because of the great variety of landscape in the beautiful area of north-west Kent which is easily accessible from Greater London. The walks take us over hills and through little secluded valleys, open downland, forestry areas, farmland, hopfields and orchards and beside rivers and lakes, mostly man-made but not the less attractive for that. We also have the opportunity to see historic buildings and many examples of fine domestic architecture of bygone centuries.

The sketch maps accompanying each walk should be an adequate supplement to the instructions in the text, but for those who wish to learn to find their way in the countryside by using a detailed map the appropriate number of the OS 1:50 000 Landranger map is given or you could use the new OS Explorer maps which are now available and are recommended.

No special equipment is needed to enjoy the countryside on foot, but do wear a stout pair of shoes and remember that at least one muddy patch is likely even on the sunniest day.

We are convinced that regular walking in the country is of untold benefit to health of mind and body. Particularly it is hoped that families when walking will encourage their children's interest in the natural world around them. The use of the wide range of inexpensive books on flora and fauna should encourage walkers to express their knowledge and assist in the identification of wild flowers, butterflies, insects, etc. Keeping quiet and being observant might well bring the added pleasure of seeing a wild deer in or near the cover of the woods, a fox running over a field, a heron alighting beside or standing motionless in water or even, on very rare occasions, seeing at a riverside the swift flash of blue of a kingfisher in flight.

Please follow the Country Code:

1. Guard against all risks of fire.
2. Fasten all gates.
3. Keep dogs under proper control.
4. Keep to the paths across farmland.
5. Avoid damaging fences.
6. Leave no litter.
7. Safeguard water supplies.
8. Protect wild life, wild plants and trees.
9. Go carefully on country roads.
10. Respect the life of the countryside.

If the use of this book manages to introduce even a few to the beauty and interest of the countryside we shall feel our labours have not been in vain.

AUDREY KRYNSKI
JANET SPAYNE

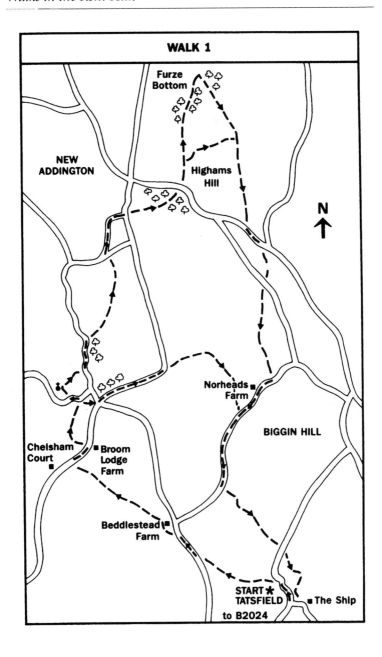

MAP: OS Landranger 187

TATSFIELD
🌿

BEDDLESTEAD, CHELSHAM CHURCH, HIGHAM'S HILL,
8 MILES OR 9 MILES; OMITTING HIGHAM'S HILL, 6 MILES

Because the vagaries of county boundaries leave Tatsfield in an enclave of Surrey surrounded by Kent, we cross the boundary several times while exploring small hills and valleys in its vicinity. There are many pleasant views and it is particularly recommended for late May when the fields and hedgerows provide a profusion of cow parsley, buttercups and bluebells.

HOW TO GET THERE: This walk starts from the village green on the south side of Tatsfield ½ mile off the B2024.

With the pond on our left we go forward, soon bearing right to the edge of the green where we continue down a road in a small housing estate. After going downhill and uphill, we turn left and immediately right on a signposted bridleway, following the hedge on our right. Later we go through a gate, continue downhill then uphill and go through another gate. From here the line of the path is forward diagonally to the corner of the field and out to the road.

We turn right and after about 300 yards turn left on a signposted bridleway bearing slightly left to go through a gate. At the crossing farm road we turn left and in a few yards right on a cart track with the buildings of Beddlestead Farm on our right. Records show this area as a manorial smallholding under the name of Bednestede as far back as the 14th century. Opposite a brick farm building we turn left through a gate and

11

go diagonally downhill to go through a gate in the valley bottom. We bear left over a shoulder of hill, making for a stile in the hedge. Turn left uphill on a fenced path. Later we go through a strip of woods and eventually reach the road where we turn right.

Opposite Broom Lodge Farm we turn left over a stile and go down the side of a field with a hedge on our left. At a hedge we cross a stile and turn right and follow it on our right to the road. We turn left for a few yards then bear right up a drive to St Leonard's church, Chelsham, situated in trees well away from its village. The original church was late Norman but the existing fabric dates mainly from its restoration in 1871.

FOR THE SHORTER VERSION: After visiting the church we turn left down the road, retracing our steps for a few yards. At the footpath sign on the right we enter the field and bear left on a waymarked path to a crossroads. We take the second road on the left and follow it for ½ mile, enjoying fine views across the valley. When the road turns left, we maintain direction on a track soon going downhill. Later we turn right on a path marked 'Biggin Hill Circular' and go downhill then uphill. At a crossing path we turn left, still uphill, with a hedge on our left and reaching the top of the hill, we bear right on a waymarked path. At a T junction we turn right on Norheads Lane for nearly ¾ mile, enjoying pleasant aspects.

FOR THE LONGER VERSIONS: With the church on our left, we go through the churchyard to a stile, cross the field diagonally right then follow the fence on our right to the road where we turn left for about ¼ mile. As the road turns left, we bear right on a track. After ½ mile we reach the road, turn right and almost immediately left, following the road as it later bends right. At a T junction we cross to a bridleway which going forward later takes us through woods and out to another road. We cross to a bridleway opposite enjoying fine views as we go along the top of Higham's Hill.

FOR THE 8 MILE WALK: Just before a house, we turn right on a signposted footpath going downhill, over a stile, then diagonally left to another stile. We now bear left on the edge of a strip of woods, following a wire fence on the left and continuing downhill. At the bottom of the valley we turn left to a gate, following the hedge on our left uphill and turning right at the top.

FOR THE 9 MILE WALK: We continue along the bridleway, later going downhill and entering woods. Crossing a stile on our right, we take a slightly visible field path, going diagonally uphill at a gentle gradient. Near the top of the slope we cross a stile and continue to a stile on the right which takes us through a shrubby area. Soon we cross a stile on our right and turn left along the hillside.

BOTH LONGER WALKS NOW CONTINUE TOGETHER: With trees on our left, we keep along the top of the hill enjoying splendid views across the valley. We continue on this path for about ½ mile, later in woods, ignoring paths turning off to houses. Finally we go downhill and down steps to the road, where we turn left for about 300 yards. After passing Crown Ash Cottage on the right, just before the main road ahead, we turn right on a downhill track. This shortly bears right, but we fork left through trees to an open field down which we continue diagonally to a footpath sign and the road.

We cross the road, continuing direction over a field to a stile after which our path gradually climbs the hill, giving good views on the right. At the top we bear left with a line of trees on our right. Later we continue forward with a fence on our right to cross a stile and turn right on a road which immediately forks. We may take either as both soon join and we continue on Norheads Lane for nearly ¾ mile.

ALL VERSIONS NOW CONTINUE TOGETHER: Just before woods ahead, we turn left on a signposted footpath, later entering woods and taking the extreme right hand path. We are soon out in the open again and bear left downhill then uphill with houses on our left. After crossing a stile in the top left hand corner, we bear slightly right with a fence on our right through a wooded area. Reaching a field we maintain direction diagonally to a stile in the corner. We turn left with a fence on our left, soon going through a gate and turning right through a gap in the hedge. Continue to the road with the remains of a hedge on the left.

A few yards to the right on the road, we cross a stile on the left and go through trees, then diagonally right down a sloping field to another stile giving access to a small path taking us up to a lane. Here we turn right, following the lane to a footpath sign, where we turn right between houses. We shortly reach the outskirts of Tatsfield's green and soon bear left passing the pond on our right.

Refreshments: The Ship at Tatsfield.

MAPS: OS Landranger 187 and 188

CUDHAM, KNOCKHOLT

5 MILES OR 7 MILES

In this walk we explore several small valleys and wooded hills which provide exceptionally fine views. Despite winter mud on some paths there is a fine array of snowdrops in and beyond Knockholt churchyard in February.

HOW TO GET THERE: For Cudham we turn south off the A21 at Green Street Green. The walk starts from a car park at playing fields just beyond Cudham church and The Blacksmith's Arms.

Leaving the car park, we turn left on the road and opposite Cudham Forge turn right on a signposted footpath leading to a lower road where we turn left for nearly ½ mile. Just beyond New Barn Farm we take a path on the left waymarked 'Berry's Green Circular', shortly crossing a stile.

FOR THE SHORTER VERSION: We soon turn left, following the hedge downhill then uphill into woods with a wire fence on our left. Our path soon leads to a waymarked stile which we cross into an enclosed path, shortly continuing between fields.

FOR THE LONGER VERSION: We continue direction along the side of a pleasant valley with trees on our right for about ½ mile, crossing two stiles en route. At a gate beside a signpost, we cross to another stile then bear slightly left uphill to a stile under a tree. After continuing uphill we maintain direction to the road.

We turn left on the road, keeping left when it forks. At a

15

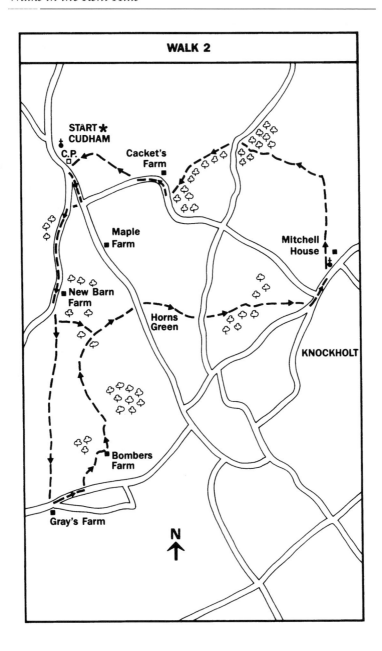

footpath signposted to Horns Green we turn left with the hedge on our left, cross a stile and head for a gap 50 yards left of telephone wires. Going over two successive stiles we bear left towards a stile and gate amongst trees into a rough lane, where we turn right. With the attractive buildings of Bombers Farm on our right, we turn left on a lane which later bends right and passes another house. Maintaining direction, we go gradually downhill and after about ½ mile come out to an open field on our left. We continue forward a few more yards passing a stile on our right then bearing right on a path into woods. This soon goes uphill and bears left. We turn right over a waymarked stile into an enclosed path which shortly continues between fields.

BOTH VERSIONS NOW CONTINUE TOGETHER: A drive brings us to the road at Horns Green. Crossing to a stile opposite, we go forward to the far right hand corner of a field, cross a stile and continue diagonally over the next field to a gate and stile. We then bear left with the hedge on our left to the road, cross to a stile opposite and go forward on a path with fencing on our right. After crossing a stile we have the fence on our left and we continue on a path just inside woods, soon leaving them to cross a stile in wire fencing. At two electricity supply poles we turn right over a stile following the path uphill to a stile with a house over on our right. Our path goes through an area of scrub and becomes fenced for a short distance. Maintaining direction over a field and stiles, through a few trees and an area of bracken, we finally reach the road.

We turn left into Knockholt village, shortly passing The Crown and turning left into the churchyard. St Katharine's church dates back to 1281 with considerable 19th-century additions and restorations. There is a 14th-century font and brass dated 1503. Passing the church on our right, we leave the churchyard by a stile, continue forward to a gateway followed by a second gateway and stile and maintain direction along the edge of fields with the hedge on our right. We then cross a waymarked stile and bear slightly left down a sloping field, continuing downhill through a strip of woods to cross a stile beside a signpost. We turn left with the hedge on our left and soon cross stiles on either side of a track. Keeping woods on our right for a short distance, we then turn left over a stile and cross a field diagonally into woods where we follow the path to the road.

We turn right past a house then left on a bridleway into woods. Two other paths turn off at the same point, but ours is the one on the extreme left. After about ¼ mile the path goes downhill and turns left with fields on our right. At a stile we turn right uphill to the road where we turn right past Cacket's Farm. Just before houses we turn right over a stile and follow a path diagonally over fields with Cudham church steeple ahead to a kissing gate. We turn left beside a wall and are soon at the playing field with a toilet block straight ahead and the car park a short distance to the left.

REFRESHMENTS: Inns at Cudham and Knockholt.

WALK 3

MAP: OS Landranger 188

KNOCKHOLT

High Wood, Pratt's Bottom,
6 miles

This walk is suitable for any time of the year. Very little mud will be encountered as we explore the woods and small valleys in this part of Kent.

How to get there: By train or bus to Knockholt station on the A21. There is a car park at the station.

From Knockholt station we cross the road and turn left for a few yards to a gate and waymarked post on the right. We follow waymarked posts through the golf course eventually reaching a hedge with a stile which we cross. Maintaining direction we have a field on the right and at the end go through a barrier and continue with a field on the left, soon reaching a road where we turn left.

Just past The Old Rectory on the left, we turn right through a gate into playing fields and bear left to cross a stile in the hedgerow. We turn right keeping trees on our right, soon going downhill. At the bottom bearing slightly right and still keeping trees on our right we soon go uphill on a wide grassy track with a field on our right and trees on our left. At the top we go forward to cross a stile taking us into a hedged footpath eventually reaching a road. We turn right down Hookwood Road, soon going through a gate and forward on a track following the line of telegraph wires. Later we turn right over a stile in fencing and go downhill with fencing on the left. We

19

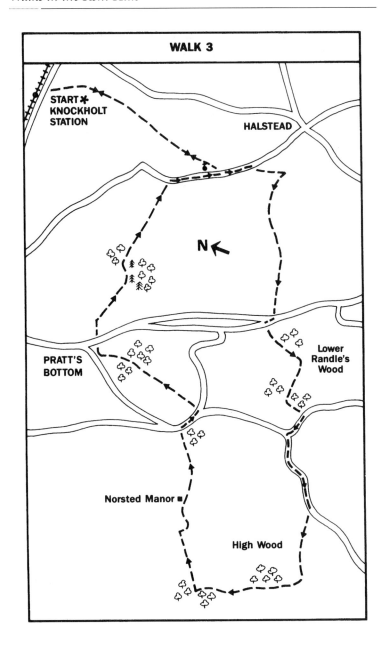

continue across the valley bottom into woods going steeply uphill. After going over a crossing path, we soon cross a stile at the edge of the wood and turn left to the road. We turn right and soon left at a T junction.

We follow this minor road for about ¼ mile ignoring a path on the right signposted to Pratt's Bottom. As the road bends left, we turn right on a signposted bridleway. Later, at a crossing track, we turn right going slightly downhill through High Wood. We continue across a pleasant valley and re-enter woodland, shortly turning right downhill with a wire fence on our left. From a kissing gate we cross an open valley slightly left going over a stile to a wide track where we turn right for a few yards then left. We pass on our left Norsted Manor, basically 13th-century but much restored, and on our right farm buildings and a row of houses.

Our track, now a surfaced lane, continues with open fields either side and finally comes out to a minor road where we turn right uphill. At a road junction we turn left over fields on an enclosed signposted bridleway which we follow for about ½ mile. Later we have woods on our right and our path goes downhill, passing sundry buildings. We maintain direction to the outskirts of Pratt's Bottom, turning right across a green to a signposted uphill footpath with a small chapel on the right and The Bull's Head on the left.

When we are nearly at the top of the hill, we turn right through a gap in the hedge and in a few yards turn left over a stile into a field. Veering slightly away from the fence on the right we cross the field to woods ahead which we enter by another stile. We follow the main path ignoring side turnings. When an open field on the left becomes visible we turn left uphill, at first with the field on our left. We continue uphill ignoring side turnings and eventually come out to a field. We continue direction over the field for about ¼ mile, finally coming out to a road where we turn right.

In a few yards we turn left through a gate into the golf course then turn right following the hedge on our right back to the waymarked post and stile we were at, at the beginning of the walk. Turning left we now follow the waymarked posts back to the road, go through the gate and turn left to cross the road back to the station.

REFRESHMENTS: The Bull's Head at Pratt's Bottom.

MAP: OS Landranger 188

OTFORD, POLHILL, SHOREHAM
❧

7 MILES; OMITTING SHOREHAM, 5½ MILES

This is an enjoyable walk for any time of the year. We see some delightful houses in Otford and Shoreham and walking along the banks of the river Darent is very pleasant. Some of the steeper paths can be slippery in wet weather.

HOW TO GET THERE: By train or bus to Otford station where there is also a car park (free at weekends and bank holidays). On Sundays there is a free unlimited-time car park opposite The Bull inn (limited to two hours on weekdays).

From the station approach we turn left to the village pond, now isolated on a traffic island. Passing the war memorial and church on our left, we take a tarmac path leading to the ruined remains of a splendid Tudor palace. In the early 16th century it belonged to the Archbishop of Canterbury and later passed to Henry VIII who once stayed there with a retinue of 4,000. Part of the palace remains have been embodied in a few cottages which stand between a tower and part of the main gatehouse, used as a dovecot in the 19th century.

We bear right past the Tudor palace and cross Palace Fields diagonally to Sevenoaks Road, continuing on a signposted footpath opposite a row of shops. There is a good view of Polhill ahead as we make our way back to the main road where we turn left.

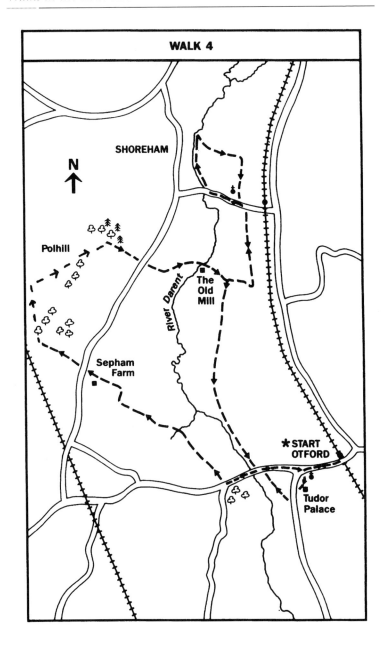

On our left we pass the ancient timbered house Pickmoss (14th to 15th-century) and Broughton Manor (16th to 17th-century). Opposite a left turning we go over a stile on the right by a bus stop and cross a field to another stile, then follow the hedge on our right. One hundred yards after the next stile, we turn left, cross a small stream and follow a path with a fence on its right. This joins a wider track taking us towards Sepham Farm. At a double electric post we turn right and soon left at a waymarked post, passing the farm on our left and orchards on our right. We continue to the road, cross to a footpath opposite and scramble up a bank to a stile. Keeping trees on our right we follow the overhead wires to another stile which takes us through a fence into the Polhill Bank Nature Reserve. We continue steeply uphill on the open hillside. This is an ideal place for a rest with splendid views, and in summer an abundance of wild flowers typical of chalk downland.

We pass through the gate in a further fence marking the upper boundary of the Nature Reserve, and enter Pilots Wood, continuing uphill until the path turns right at the motorway cutting. We do not cross the footbridge over the motorway, but continue with the motorway on our left until very soon we bear half-right at a waymarked fork. After about ½ mile, immediately after a crossing path, a stile on the right gives access to the open hillside. Cross the sloping field diagonally, going down the hill. Reaching the other side of the field we turn right and continue downhill with the edge of the field on our left until we come to a stile and wider track taking us down to the road. We cross to the lane opposite soon passing Kennel Cottage, an historic building of Kent, where the lane becomes a path. The stream on our right is a tributary of the Darent. We soon cross the river by a footbridge, after which the path again becomes a lane, and shortly pass The Old Mill, with its beautiful garden and mill pond.

FOR THE SHORTER VERSION OMITTING SHOREHAM: We shortly turn right on a footpath signposted to Otford and follow this clear path for just over 1 mile. We pass some charming houses and Mill House and reach the road, where we turn left through the village to the station.

TO CONTINUE THE WALK TO SHOREHAM: After ¼ mile on this gently rising tarmac track, we turn left on a signposted footpath, enclosed in parts, and in ½ mile reach the road.

We turn left and are soon in the picturesque village of Shoreham. Before reaching the bridge over the river Darent, you may care to visit the church by turning right opposite the Olde George Inn. St Peter and St Paul's church dates from the early 16th century and was largely restored in the mid 19th century.

At the river bridge, we should turn right, keeping the river on our left, but a short diversion across the bridge will enable us to see more of Shoreham. Returning over the bridge, we turn left passing on our right several houses of character including Water House, where the artist Samuel Palmer used to live. We continue direction on a drive which soon becomes a footpath. The path ends at a bridge on our left but we turn right on an enclosed footpath and soon right again over a stile to a well-defined field footpath. This takes us over a small tributary, and we continue on an enclosed footpath to a crossing track. Here we turn right, keeping along the edge of a field with the hedgerow and later the churchyard wall on our right. At the road we turn left retracing an earlier part of the walk but, in reverse, the views are different. We soon turn right on the enclosed footpath back to the tarmac track where we turn right. After 150 yards we turn left on a footpath signposted to Otford and follow the directions for the shorter version.

REFRESHMENTS: Inns and tearooms in Otford. Inns in Shoreham.

MAP: OS Landranger 188

ROMNEY STREET, KEMSING
🌿

5¾ MILES OR 7 MILES

This is a beautiful walk through woodland and small valleys with many pleasant aspects and a sight of the picturesque old part of Kemsing village. It is recommended for any time of year but particularly in May when there will be an abundance of bluebells, or in autumn when the beech woods will be ablaze with colour. In wet weather some steep paths will be dangerously slippery.

HOW TO GET THERE: By train or bus to Shoreham station, where there is also a car park.

From the station approach at Shoreham station we cross the road diagonally right to a signposted footpath and go uphill on an enclosed track, soon taking the left one of two footpaths. We are soon in woods and, ignoring side turnings, we later go steeply uphill to a crossing track. Continuing direction over this track we soon bear left and come out to an open field.

We cross diagonally left to the end of Dunstall Farm buildings, round which we bear right then immediately left on a cart track passing a barn on our left. After going downhill and then uphill, as soon as the path flattens we cross a stile and bear left across two fields on a well-defined path. We go through a strip of woods on a downhill footpath out to open hillside, then bear diagonally left to cross the bottom of the valley. After a stile

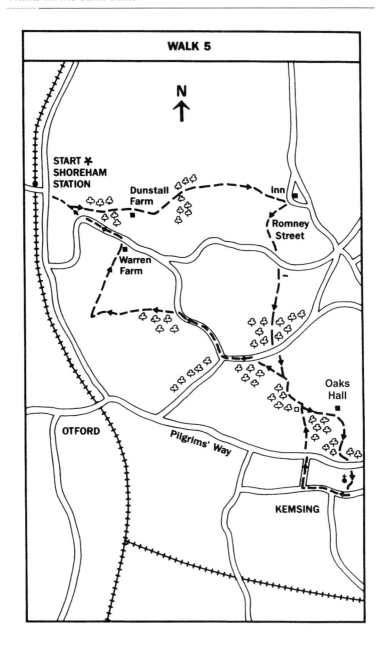

in a hedge on our right we continue direction uphill with the hedge and later a fence on our left. We go over stiles at the top of the hill, forward over a field, pass the end of a hedgerow on our right and keep diagonally right uphill with a clump of trees on our right. As our path flattens, we continue over a stile, passing a garden fence on our left to The Fox and Hounds, Romney Street.

Opposite the inn we turn right over a stile and cross the field diagonally right on a path to another stile in the hedgerow. We cross this and turn left soon going over a waymarked stile and bearing left with the hedgerow on our left. As the field ends, we go under telegraph wires and cross a stile with a red disc to continue with a hedge on the right. Another stile takes us into an enclosed footpath and we go down to the road.

We turn left up the road for a few yards then right over a stile and *straight* up the field, soon passing a fenced hollow over on our right and going through a gap in trees. Following the fence on our right down to a stile we continue to the open hillside. We bear left downhill to a stile which takes us to a gently rising path through woods for ¼ mile. At the road we turn left and soon right on a drive. Later we bear left and just before Oaks Hall gates we turn right over a stile and skirt two sides of a field on an enclosed footpath. We finally turn right downhill into trees and bear left to the open hillside above the outskirts of Kemsing, near a seat from which we can admire the view.

FOR THE LONGER VERSION: A few yards downhill from the seat, we turn left on a small but well-defined path which twists and turns along the hillside affording fine views and, in summer, a variety of wild flowers. We continue on over a stile and later take the right hand track going slightly downhill. After another stile and several kissing gates we come out to the open hillside again. With a seat up on our left, we continue downhill over grass to a gate in a fenced strip of trees. Here we turn left for about 30 yards to go through a similar gate and down to the road. We turn left for 100 yards then right on a path leading into a recreation ground, going downhill to the corner where we turn right with the church on our right.

From the church we go forward down Church Lane, turning right down the High Street and passing numerous beautiful and ancient houses, a shop or two, St Edith Hall, built in 1911, two public houses and St Edith's Well. Ignoring a road turning off on the left at the well, we maintain direction past a few shops, turning right up The Landway, a residential road sloping gradually uphill to the main road.

A signposted footpath to the right takes us to a narrow path on the left. We bear right, shortly turning right onto a wide path continuing uphill, through woodland and a stepped path, soon coming to more open hillside and reaching the seat overlooking Kemsing.

BOTH WALKS NOW FOLLOW THE SAME ROUTE: We will be retracing an earlier part of the walk for the next ¼ mile, and go steeply uphill through trees, coming out to the enclosed footpath and following it back to Oaks Hall drive. On this we bear left, then right, and opposite a house we turn left on a path with many kissing gates which we follow over fields to the road.

We turn left and are soon at a road junction where we turn right on the road signposted to Shoreham. After about ½ mile, as the road bends right, we turn left over a stile on a signposted footpath keeping the fence on our right and later continuing on a track through woods. We come out to the open hillside with fine views of Otford, Dunton Green and Chipstead Water in the far distance. Maintaining direction our path soon re-enters woods, goes slightly downhill and emerges again on an open hillside where we turn right. Once more our path enters woods, and at a waymarked post we fork left steeply downhill, soon coming out into the open and continuing round the hillside. Our path bears right steeply uphill and shortly bears right again up to a stile and open field. (The steep downhill and uphill path can be avoided by taking an unofficial path on the right by the waymarked post, keeping along the contour till we meet a steep path joining on the left. Here we bear right up to a stile and open field.)

We go forward diagonally uphill bearing away from woods on our left, cross a stile in fencing, continue direction towards a farm area, then cross another stile and follow the drive to a road.

After turning left for about 200 yards we take a signposted bridleway on the right at a bend in the road, go downhill through woods and finally retrace our steps to the station.

REFRESHMENTS: Romney Street and Kemsing.

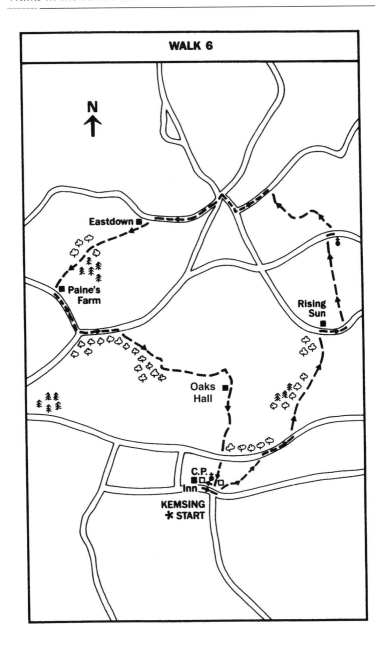

MAP: OS Landranger 188

KEMSING, WOODLANDS
🌿

5 MILES

Starting in the village of Kemsing and exploring parts of the North Downs, this walk inevitably includes uphill stretches, but with gentle gradient, and amply compensated by splendid hillside views. Concentration is necessary as our walk is not well waymarked and crosses and recrosses three other well waymarked routes.

HOW TO GET THERE: Kemsing is on a minor road 2 miles east of Otford. The walk starts from the village car park which is just off the High Street behind The Wheatsheaf inn car park.

From the car park we turn left up the High Street past St Edith Hall then left up Church Lane. Opposite the churchyard entrance we turn right and cross the recreation ground diagonally, keeping to the left of the small wood in the centre, and head for the gap in the hedge along the top boundary. We pass through this gap and continue to the right along the enclosed path beside the road until a gap on the left gives access to the road, where we continue direction for a short distance. Beside the drive of a house named Woodlea, we turn left on a signposted uphill footpath. On crossing a stile to the open hillside we bear diagonally left up to two successive stiles. We then bear right uphill, cross a stile in the corner, turn right on a path to the next stile, then turn left with trees on our left to another stile in the corner. We now keep the hedgerow on our right and cross two more stiles to reach the road opposite The Rising Sun where we turn right.

Opposite a building on the right, we turn left over a stile and cross a field to a stile into woods. On leaving the woods we cross a golf fairway to a stile, then follow the hedge on our right to the road beside the Woodlands church, built in 1851-2 and well worth visiting. Turning right for about 30 yards, we then turn left over a stile beside a gate and go up a field with trees on our right. At another stile and gate we turn left with a fence on the left. Reaching a few trees ahead, we turn right over a golf fairway soon continuing with trees on our right. We pass through a gate, continue across a golf fairway, and pass through a gap in trees. We turn left along the edge of another golf fairway for about 50 yards, then turn half-right and cross several golf fairways, passing a pond with a group of yellow marker posts. In the wooded corner of the golf course with trees on our right we drop down through a gap in the trees ahead to reach a lane where we turn left.

At the T junction we turn right, shortly turning left at the crossroads and soon right at a fork. Just before a house called Eastdown, we turn left over a stile and turn right going behind the house, then cross the field diagonally to a stile in the far left hand corner. This takes us through a strip of woods and out to the open hillside with fine views across a small valley. We go downhill slightly left over the valley bottom, soon entering woods over a stile. After about ¼ mile we leave the woods and follow the fence on our left over stiles to the road where we turn left past Paine's Farm.

At a road junction we turn left and soon right over a stile on part of the North Downs Way, eventually coming out on a drive where we turn right, soon bearing left leaving the North Downs Way which goes over a stile to the right, and passing between the gateposts of Oaks Hall. We follow the drive to a stile on the left, turn right parallel with the drive, then bear left over a stile into the next field which we cross diagonally to reach an isolated stile where the fence has been removed. We turn right here and at a telegraph pole we bear left to cross a stile and follow a hedged path, continuing over a drive with Oaks Hall on our right. We go downhill on a narrow path finally reaching the open hillside above Kemsing where we turn left on a path which later ends on a grassy slope. Bearing right downhill we pass through two gates about 30 yards apart and continue down to the road. We cross to a footpath slightly left, continue down the recreation ground and bear right through the churchyard to a tarmac path with an opening into the car park.

REFRESHMENTS: The Rising Sun en route. Inns at Kemsing.

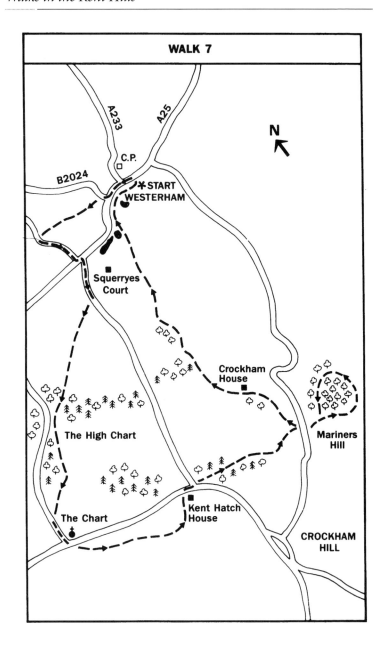

· · · · · · · · · ·
WALK 7
· · · · · · · · · ·

MAPS: OS Landranger 187 and 188

WESTERHAM
ᔛ

FARLEY COMMON, HIGH CHART, THE CHART,
CROCKHAM HILL COMMON, MARINERS HILL, SQUERRYES
PARK, 7 MILES OMITTING MARINERS HILL, 6 MILES

*This is a walk through parkland and open woodland, with an
opportunity to visit Chartwell. The walk is particularly
recommended in winter or spring, before the trees are in full leaf.*

HOW TO GET THERE: By car on the A25 or A233. There is a car
park just off the A233. An infrequent bus service.

We leave the centre of Westerham turning right on the B2024
signposted Croydon and immediately left through posts down
a tarmac path leading into Westbury Terrace. We continue
forward and shortly maintain direction on a signposted
footpath, soon ignoring a right turning. At Farley Common we
continue direction on a tarmac drive with the common on our
right, at the end of which we turn left doubling back downhill.
In less than ¼ mile we are at the main road. We turn left for a
few yards then right on another road, passing on our left a
picturesque row of cottages and the lodge of Squerryes Court,
a manor house built in 1681 and open to the public during the
summer months. As we continue up the road Squerryes lake
and the house beyond can be seen on the left before we turn
right on a farm road opposite the house drive.

Just before reaching a timbered house on the right, and just
after a telegraph pole, we turn left over a ditch and stile and bear
right along the edge of a field keeping parallel with the road. We

go over a stile and slightly uphill with a hedge on our right, enjoying pleasant aspects.

As the field ends, we cross a stile and go forward into woods on a small path which soon takes us over a crossing track. We are now on the edge of The High Chart and we continue direction eventually reaching a wide bridleway with the road nearby on the right. Here we turn left and almost immediately take the second of two uphill tracks turning off on the right, leading us to a wide forestry track where we turn right. Later bearing left our track is joined by another major track coming in on the right. We take a waymarked path with a seat beside it, passing a pond on the left. We take the right hand waymarked path going uphill, reaching a crossing track as it flattens out. We continue ahead beneath pine trees, shortly joining a path coming in from the left. Maintain direction for a short distance then take the grassy path in a more open area. We bear diagonally left towards the church steeple visible ahead and soon reach the road. The Carpenter's Arms is over to the right.

If we are not visiting the inn, we turn left down the road, passing the Limpsfield Chart church before we cross the main road to a signposted bridleway, initially with a tarmac surface. Opposite an old schoolhouse we turn left into trees and have good views on our right. After about ½ mile we turn right on a tarmac drive following it until we reach the gates of Scearn Bank House. We turn left and go steeply uphill reaching a junction of paths where we take the right hand path into trees. Here we bear left on a surfaced drive and soon come out at the road where we turn right for a short distance passing Kent Hatch House on our right.

We cross the road to a postbox just past a road turning off on the left and take a waymarked path into woods, bearing slightly right. We go over a crossing path and at the next crossing path turn right. We are now on the Greensand Way and follow the waymarks for some time. We finally emerge in a clearing in front of a house, The Warren. With the house on our right, we go straight ahead, soon going through silver birches.

We continue downhill through woods and at the bottom our path merges with other paths from left and right.

FOR THE SHORTER VERSION: We turn left.

FOR THE LONGER VERSION: We bear right for a short distance on an uphill drive to the road, which we cross to a footpath opposite signposted 'Greensand Way', on the right of a private drive, and go steeply uphill. Passing a house and fence on our right, we keep to the footpath on the extreme right (the Greensand Way goes off to the left) with the open space of Mariners Hill on our right. After about ¼ mile our path merges into a wider track joining from the left. Just before the path bears left and goes steeply downhill to the road, we turn left on a slightly rising path through a bar gate taking us round the hillside.

We stay on this path for about ⅓ mile enjoying fine views of the Chartwell estate down on our right and Toy's Hill beyond.

If we wish to visit Chartwell, the former home of Sir Winston Churchill, now in the care of the National Trust, we continue ahead for a few yards and turn right to go steeply downhill on a stepped path to the road and the entrance to Chartwell opposite. Chartwell is open to the public from March to the end of June and 1st September to 31st October daily, except Monday and Tuesday. In July and August it is open daily.

If not visiting Chartwell, we bear left for a few yards then turn left on an uphill path and once again we are on the Greensand Way and follow the waymarks to the house and fence we passed earlier, continuing forward and downhill to the road. We cross to April Cottage drive opposite and go downhill to a junction of paths where we take the one on the extreme right.

BOTH WALKS NOW FOLLOW THE SAME ROUTE: We continue for about ¼ mile with the slopes of Crockham Hill Common rising on our left. Just past the garden of Crockham House on our right, we go over a stile and forward to another stile with a wooded hill with ancient earthworks on our left. When these woods end we continue forward on a wide cart track uphill. Beyond the top there is an open gateway on the left and we turn right over a stile to go through a few trees to another stile, and cross a field to two more stiles in quick succession. We soon bear right downhill to a lodge where a final stile brings us into a drive on which we turn left with a small lake on our left and the river on our right. Just past a footbridge on our right we bear right on a path passing a beautiful cottage on our left and, going uphill to a stile, we are shortly out to a small road. We cross to an enclosed footpath which finally turns left through the King's Arms car park and brings us to a bus stop and the main road of Westerham opposite The George and Dragon.

REFRESHMENTS: Westerham where there are several inns and tea shops and The Carpenter's Arms at Limpsfield Chart. Also at Chartwell.

············
WALK 8
············

MAP: OS Landranger 188

TOY'S HILL, MARINERS HILL, CROCKHAM HILL
❧

4 MILES OR 7 MILES

This walk starts at nearly 800 ft and takes us down to the farming area below the hills, returning by gentle gradients. We see some fine houses built to catch the views from the sandstone ridge above the Weald.

HOW TO GET THERE: By car to the National Trust car park at Toy's Hill taking the A25 and turning south at Brasted. The car park is on the right just beyond The Fox and Hounds.

With our backs to the road, we go up some steps in the rear left hand corner of the car park, following a well-defined path to a junction of paths. We bear left, soon avoiding a left fork, going downhill and eventually reaching the road.

FOR THE SHORTER VERSION: We turn right on the road and are soon at a viewpoint with seats, an extensive view over the Weald and an old well which was provided in 1898 for the Toy's Hill inhabitants by Octavia Hill, co-founder of the National Trust. About 60 yards or so beyond this we turn left on a drive beside a house called Bardogs, soon continuing on a footpath on the left. The path turns left then right and goes downhill, finally taking us over a stile to a field. We go downhill with trees on our right and at the corner of the field bear right into woods, taking

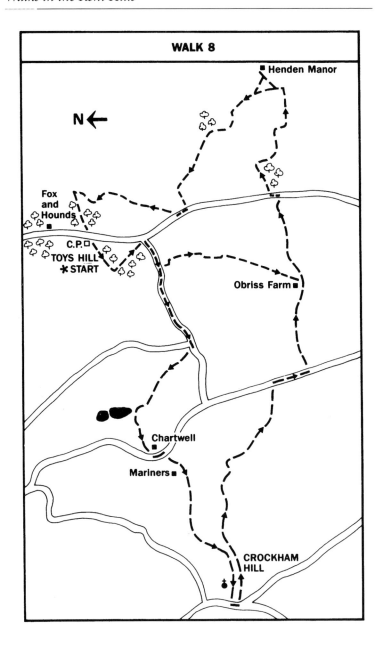

WALK 8

Henden Manor

N ←

Fox
and
Hounds

C.P.
TOYS HILL
✳ START

Obriss Farm

Chartwell

Mariners ■

CROCKHAM
HILL

the left hand one of two stiles. Shortly we are out in a field and go forward into the next field. We continue diagonally to some yards left of the far right hand corner, where we cross a stile and keep the hedge on our right. Soon we pass the buildings of Obriss Farm and a gate across a farm track on our right.

FOR THE LONGER VERSION: We turn right for about ½ mile and just beyond a road turning off on the right we turn right on a wide footpath. After following this fenced track for over ¼ mile we cross a stile into the Chartwell Farm area, bear left through a kissing gate beside oast houses and soon bear left on a drive. At the road we turn left and soon right on a signposted footpath at a kissing gate beside a lodge. We go forward on a drive on the south side of Mariners Hill, passing the beautiful house and gardens of Mariners and continuing through a gate. Maintaining direction for about ¼ mile, when the drive turns right at an oast house incorporated into an attractive residence, we turn left on a signposted footpath to Crockham Hill church going down steps between the gardens of houses clinging to the hillside. We cross a stile and follow the hedge on our right to a bridge and gate in the field corner, and go forward over a field soon with a churchyard on our right. After another gate we pass the Crockham Hill church and village school on our right as we continue forward to the road. Holy Trinity church was built in 1842, entirely of local stone. Octavia Hill's grave (1838-1912) is under a yew tree on the right of the church entrance.

Turning left on the road through Crockham Hill village, we soon pass the post office. Opposite is a little public garden with seats, while The Royal Oak is a little further down the road. Just beyond the post office we turn left on a private road.

After about ½ mile at a beautiful tile hung house we turn left uphill and later bear right on the drive of Chandlers. We shortly leave the drive at a gate on the left and follow a wide, hedged track which circles round a fine house and garden, Coachmans, on our right. We go downhill beside the house enjoying splendid views, cross a stile and go slightly left downhill to another stile in the field corner, maintaining direction slightly uphill over the next field to the far left hand corner. A stile takes us through a strip of woods and we continue with trees on our right to another stile which soon brings us to the road.

We turn right for about 200 yards then left on a gated track leading to Obriss Farm. Passing the farm on our left, we continue over a stile beside a gate.

BOTH VERSIONS NOW CONTINUE TOGETHER: With our backs to the gate we bear diagonally left across the field making for a stile and gate about halfway along the opposite fence and just beyond a few willows. After crossing it we follow the hedge on our right, through a gate and strip of woods to a gate and maintain direction over a field to a stile onto a wooded track where we bear right on a path to the road.

Turning left for a short distance, we then turn right on the Tan House Farm track which later turns right. After passing the farm, we cross a stream and continue direction on an uphill hedged track. As the track ends, we ignore a stile ahead and turn left for a few yards to a gate and continue over a field making for a gate on the left of a line of trees. We turn left on a lane soon passing a house and turning on the left, going forward to look at some oast houses converted into picturesque cottages. (Henden Manor, an attractive 16th-century or earlier moated manor house, much restored, is just ahead but not very visible.) Retracing our steps, we take the surfaced track with the oast house cottages on our right, soon joined by another track feeding in on the left.

We remain on the concrete farm track till it ends, when we cross a stile by the right hand one of two gates. Follow the track shortly turning left downhill to a gate ahead. Beyond the gate we follow a tree lined track for about 80 yards then bear left over the field to the widest of three openings in the hedge opposite. We continue direction to a stile ahead, go through a belt of trees and bear diagonally uphill and through some freestanding trees to a stile and gate in the top left hand corner.

After crossing the stile we follow the track, avoid a left fork and soon reach the road where we turn right uphill.

In rather less than ¼ mile, we reach a road junction and turn right down Scords Lane. Later this turns right but we maintain direction and take a track forking left uphill. At a junction of paths we turn left and at a crossing track we turn left and left again on a track with a red and green waymark, keeping right, then left, which brings us out opposite the car park.

REFRESHMENTS: The Fox and Hounds at Toy's Hill. The Royal Oak in Crockham Hill.

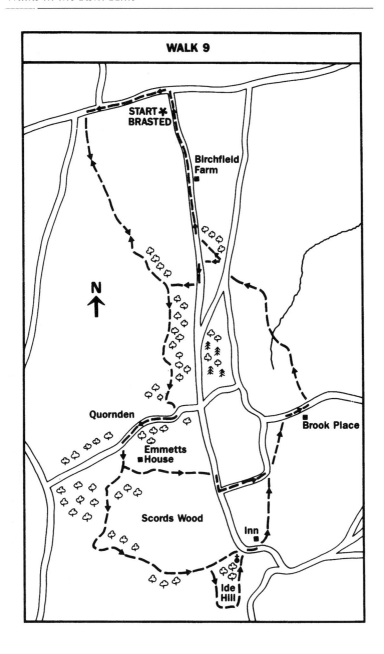

MAP: OS Landranger 188

BRASTED
❧

SCORDS WOOD, IDE HILL, 7 MILES
SCORDS WOOD, EMMETTS, 5½ MILES

This is a suitable walk for any time of the year, with good views and an opportunity to visit Emmetts Garden, owned by the National Trust.

HOW TO GET THERE: By bus to Brasted (limited service). By car on the A25 with limited parking in the main street.

From the centre of Brasted near the pedestrian crossing we turn up Elliotts Lane, which soon becomes a footpath. After ½ mile we pass a few cottages on the right and when the track bears right into farm buildings marked Charlfield Farm we keep left on a bridleway with woods on our left. Later we ignore left turnings and continue slightly uphill. We cross a stile with a field on our right and Charman's Wood on the left. Finally, opposite the buildings of Quornden Farm, we turn sharply left uphill to another stile and ignoring an immediate left path we continue to the road where we turn right for ¼ mile.

Opposite a house on the right, Beech Lodge, we turn left on a bridleway into Scords Wood and bearing right we continue to a crossing track.

FOR THE SHORTER VERSION: We turn left on the crossing track and soon go over a stile into Emmetts Garden, open April to October, Wednesday to Sunday in the afternoon. With a good view of Bough Beech Reservoir on the right, we follow the drive down to the road where we turn right and take the first turning on the left. After ¼ mile this turns sharply left but we continue on a signposted footpath skirting the garden of a bungalow called The Ramblers.

FOR THE LONGER VERSION: At the crossing track we keep forward and continue to a major crossing track, Weardale Way, where we go uphill with a steep drop on the left (there is a good mud-avoidance path on the left). Ignoring minor crossing paths, we maintain direction for ¼ mile to a red waymarked crossing track where we turn left. Soon we pass a house on our right and take the right fork down to a stile and open fields. Here we turn left.

We are soon at the corner of woods, where we bear right down to a gate and stile, continue forward to cross a bridge and turn left uphill towards Ide Hill church. Near the top we cross a stile and at once turn right over another stile to take a small path round the side of Ide Hill, with fine views on our right. We continue into woods and we soon cross two small streams and continue uphill. At a fork we keep left steeply uphill, emerging into a clearing near the top of the hill.

From the clearing we make for the top of the hill and follow the track out to Ide Hill village green. We cross the green to The Cock Inn which we pass as we continue down a minor road on the left of the main road. This soon turns left and ends as a residential cul-de-sac with a signposted footpath. We go over the stile and cross a sloping field on a well-defined footpath enjoying pleasant aspects. A stile brings us out near the road at a bungalow called The Ramblers, where we take a sharp turn right skirting the garden, to a signposted footpath.

BOTH VERSIONS NOW CONTINUE TOGETHER: We cross a stile and continue over fields, following the fence on our left to the road.

We turn right soon passing Brook Cottage and Brook Place with its stream fed by local springs. Opposite a barn we turn left on a track and, passing on our right a row of brick houses and avoiding a well-defined footpath on the right, we continue forward with the stream over on our left among the trees. Maintaining direction into the next field, we go under overhead wires and bear left downhill into trees. We soon turn left over the stream and then turn right on a rising path. When we emerge into an open field, we bear left uphill to a stile in the hedge. There is usually no footpath visible on the ground but we bear diagonally right to the highest part of the field, looking back to admire the view. We maintain direction to a stile, finally coming out to the road.

We have the choice of two different endings:

1. We turn right for rather less than 100 yards to a path on the left, keeping straight ahead to another road where we turn left for a short distance. At a signposted bridleway we turn right for about 300 yards, then we turn right to retrace our steps on the path we used at the beginning of the walk, following it for 1 mile back to the centre of Brasted.

2. This is shorter by ¼ mile but involves road walking: we turn right for rather less than 100 yards to a path on the left, soon forking right beside a chestnut plantation. At a road we turn right for just over ½ mile to the main road (A25) where we turn left for about ¼ mile to The White Hart at Brasted.

REFRESHMENTS: Choice of inns at Ide Hill and Brasted.

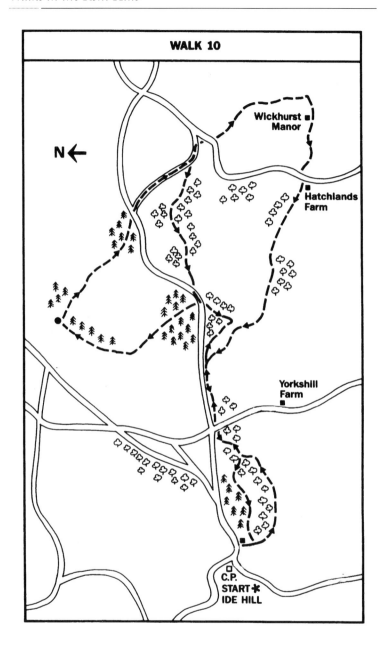

WALK 10

N ←

Wickhurst
Manor ■

■ Hatchlands
Farm

Yorkshill
Farm ■

C.P.
START ✱
IDE HILL

· · · · · · · · · · ·
WALK 10
· · · · · · · · · · ·

MAP: OS Landranger 188

IDE HILL
❧

HANGING BANK, SHEEPHILL WOOD, WICKHURST MANOR,
6 MILES; HANGING BANK, SHEEPHILL WOOD,
EVERLANDS, 5 MILES

This is a walk for any time of the year in pleasant open woodland, through farm fields with extensive views over Bough Beech Reservoir and in sight of some very attractive houses.

HOW TO GET THERE: Limited bus service to Ide Hill. By car on the A25 turning south at Sundridge for 3 miles.

Starting from the car park behind Ide Hill village hall on the B2042 turn left to go down a small side road and take the left hand higher path which leads us around the hillside known as Hanging Bank. We are soon at a junction of paths in a clearing, and take the second path on the left. Keep to the main path to a crossing track where we turn right. We continue on with a drop on our right, finally coming out to a car park and picnic area at the Yorkshill crossroads.

Maintaining direction we cross the Yorkshill road and remain parallel with the road on our left as we continue through open woods. Later our path again touches the road by a small car parking area and we continue forward on an uphill path, which bears away from the road, soon with a steep drop on our right. Our path finally turns sharply left, narrows and keeping right takes us back to the road, which we cross to a footpath opposite.

We now enter a conifer plantation, Sheephill Wood, on a small path which twists and turns till we go down to a wider track where we turn left. Going over a crossing track, we continue downhill, cross another track and go uphill. At the top we ignore a turning on the left and keep forward, later passing a turning on the right and eventually coming out in a large clearing with a junction of paths and a static water tank.

We take the path immediately on our right and turn right on a narrow path thus doubling back somewhat. Later we go downhill, and at a grassy crossing track keep right soon going over a stile. Passing a cottage on the left we take a small footpath on the left, go over a crossing track and continue uphill. Eventually we emerge on a forestry track where we turn right and downhill to the road.

We turn left for a short distance then right on a minor road with pleasant aspects. Later, the road goes uphill and we pass on our right the drive of Everlands.

FOR THE SHORTER VERSION: We go over the stile at the side of the drive, soon with coppiced chestnuts on the right of our track and open aspects on our left. The path drops down to a tarmac drive where we turn left after passing a lodge on our right and reaching the road. Turning left for a few yards, we turn left again on a footpath into woods, almost at once ignoring a path on the right. We are now retracing an earlier part of the walk. When we reach the edge of an escarpment with fine views, our path bears right and gradually takes us back to the car park and picnic area at the Yorkshill crossroads.

FOR THE LONGER VERSION: About 60 yards beyond the Everlands drive, we turn right on a drive to a red brick house with a stone footpath sign beneath a holly tree and immediately turn left on an enclosed footpath taking us down to a lower road. We turn right for a few yards to another downhill footpath on the left. Continuing on a surfaced drive, we go through a gate and bear left. Later, after passing the second of two entrances to Wickhurst Manor, we turn right on a surfaced track. We pass the front of the 15th-century manor house and farm buildings and opposite a barn cross a stile on our left to take a signposted footpath following the waymarks and coming out to the road where we turn left.

In a few yards we turn right over a stile with Hatchlands Farm on our left, soon crossing a plank bridge and bearing left to a stile taking us into a field where we turn right. After about 200 yards we bear diagonally left over the field to a stile in trees ahead, crossing a ditch by an earth bridge and noticing the house, Everlands, higher up the slope on our right. We go through a small wood and on emerging we keep slightly left of a telegraph pole at the top of the hill. After crossing a stile at the side of a gate we continue with woods on our right. As the field tapers to a corner, we go over a stile and forward on an enclosed footpath. Later our path gradually goes uphill and eventually we come to a crossing path where we turn left, soon reaching the road by a small car parking area. We continue on, re-entering woods and retracing an earlier part of the walk until we reach the Yorkshill road.

BOTH WALKS NOW FOLLOW THE SAME ROUTE: We cross the Yorkshill road, go through the small car parking space, soon ignoring a waymarked left turning and continuing to a fork where we keep left. Shortly, at the next fork, we keep right on a mainly tree fringed path higher than the one we used earlier in the walk. Later, we have a fence and a drop on our left and our path bears right, soon joining a wider track at a lower level. We turn left on this lower track, thus doubling back for a short distance, and continue on downhill to a junction of paths with a patch of grass in the centre. We take the path on our right and retrace our steps back to the main road. We continue forward bearing right uphill for Ide Hill village, or bearing left for the small car park behind the village hall.

REFRESHMENTS: Ide Hill where there is a choice of inns.

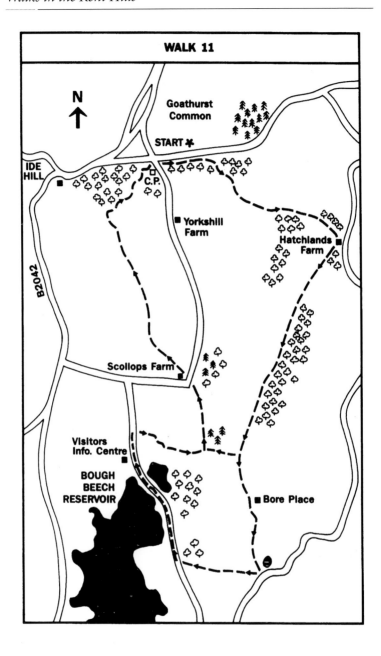

MAP: OS Landranger 188

YORKSHILL, BORE PLACE, BOUGH BEECH RESERVOIR

❧

6 MILES

FIELD WALK OMITTING BORE PLACE AND THE RESERVOIR,
4½ MILES

This is an interesting walk taking us downhill through pasture and farmland to the pleasantly landscaped Bough Beech Reservoir. In winter or after heavy rain the low lying fields may be waterlogged and very muddy.

HOW TO GET THERE: By bus (not Sundays). By car to Ide Hill on the A25 turning south at Sundridge for 3 miles.

This walk starts from a car parking space at the Yorkshill crossroads where the bus stops, and can easily be reached by turning eastwards out of Ide Hill village on the B2042 and taking the first right fork. The car park and picnic area is on the right at the crossroads near a house called Keepers on the left.

From the car park we cross the minor road through posts taking the left fork parallel with the road on the left. We keep to the main path which soon bears left towards the road and continuing parallel with the road for a few yards, we then take a stepped footpath forking right downhill: there is a waymark on a tree.

Eventually, with a wire fence and field on our right, we go over a stile to continue direction along the top of a sloping field with woods on our left. After crossing a stile at the side of a gate, we go forward bearing slightly right downhill, under telegraph wires, maintaining direction into woods. Leaving the woods, we cross the field diagonally making for a stile visible against trees and with these on our left, we continue towards Hatchlands Farm.

At the end of the trees and at a stile on our left, we turn right with farm buildings on our left and go forward slightly right to the corner of a wire fence, then bear left to cross two stiles and a stream. We bear left round the field and continue with the stream and fence on our left. At the end of the field we turn left on a track, immediately cross another stile on the right and go diagonally up to the corner of the woods. Keeping the woods on our left in this field, after crossing a stile we continue through the centre of the next field to a stile visible in the hedge ahead. We cross a stream and with a house visible ahead, at a telegraph pole, we bear right over a stile into a lane.

FOR THE SHORTER VERSION: We turn right and immediately left and follow the lane for ½ mile until we reach a minor road.

FOR THE LONGER VERSION: We turn left along the lane and later pass on our left Bore Place, dating back to the 15th century or even earlier. Bearing left through farm buildings, after about ¼ mile we come out to the road and take a stile on the right beside The Old Forge, built in 1745. With the garden hedge on our right we go up the field to another stile, then continue direction with a wire fence on our right. When this ends, we keep forward to the highest part of the field then go slightly downhill making for a stile in the bottom right hand corner. This brings us to the road, where we turn right and are soon passing the Bough Beech Reservoir, the borders of which have been made into a nature reserve.

We leave the water behind and pass on the left the entrance

to the Bough Beech visitors' centre, open April to October on Wednesdays, Saturdays and Sundays. It includes a shop, toilets and a small museum and is well worth visiting. Continuing up the road, soon after passing the last house we turn right on a signposted footpath and go forward with the hedge on our right to cross a small stream in a belt of trees. We continue direction up a sloping field making for a gap in the trees ahead. Once inside the wood, we turn left on a clear wide track and after about ¼ mile reach a minor road.

BOTH VERSIONS NOW CONTINUE TOGETHER: We turn right for a few yards then left on a signposted footpath (the sign is low down almost hidden by the hedge) with a couple of red brick houses on our right. We go through a gate, soon over a stile then turn left and maintain direction with the hedgerow on our right. Shortly, we enter a strip of woods, go over a stream on a footbridge and out to another field. We follow the hedge uphill to a gap at the top of the field. There is a yellow waymark on a post to the right of the gap and we go forward through the next field keeping the hedgerow on our right, then turning left for a few yards at the end to cross a stile. We go over the centre of a field to a strip of woods then diagonally left over the next field to a gap in the far left hand corner. We continue up the next field with woods on our left, turn left at the corner and forward for a few yards to a drive where we turn right uphill past a house.

As the drive bears left, we turn sharply right and take the bridleway which goes uphill and eventually we reach the car park area at the Yorkshill crossroads.

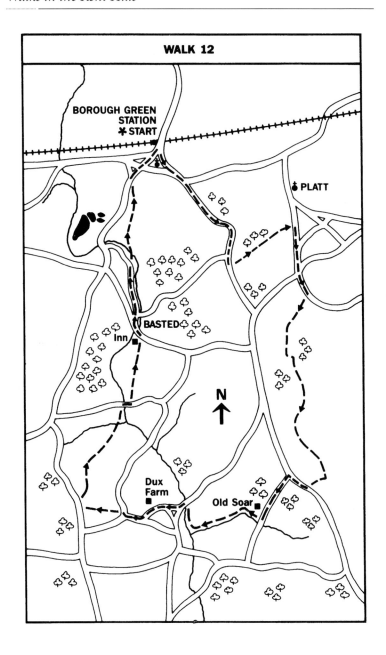

WALK 12

BOROUGH GREEN
STATION
✱ START

♂ PLATT

BASTED

Inn ■

N ↑

Dux
Farm
■

Old Soar ■

MAP: OS Landranger 188

BOROUGH GREEN
❧

PLATT, OLD SOAR MANOR, BASTED, 7½ MILES

Among orchards and farms, this walk provides a wide expanse of views and the chance to see some beautiful period houses, including the remains of an early medieval manor house.

HOW TO GET THERE: This walk starts from the car park adjoining Borough Green station on the A227. There is a smaller car park nearby on the south side of Western Road.

From Borough Green station we turn right over the railway, immediately left down Station Road and left for a short distance on the A25. We turn right on Crouch Lane for over ½ mile, then turn left on a wide signposted bridleway, initially surfaced. Later we have a hedge on our right and with Platt church over on our left, we reach the road and turn right passing some attractive old houses. After ¼ mile we continue over crossroads on a hedged lane. When this bends left we maintain direction on the second of two bridleways on the right, remaining on it for about ½ mile.

When the open area on the left gives way to woods we have wire fencing on our right. Following this to a corner, we turn right with the fencing. We cross a stile and go forward towards a clump of tall trees. Keeping the trees on our right we follow signs to a gate into a wider track which we cross slightly left to follow a waymarked path through woods. Eventually at a crossing track we turn right downhill to a road where we turn right.

We shortly turn left on a minor road and soon pass Old Soar

Manor, the remains of an early medieval manor house belonging to the National Trust and in the care of English Heritage (open daily to the public in summer months). Continuing to the bottom of the hill, we turn right on a signposted footpath following a small stream on the left and soon bearing left with the stream. After crossing a stile and ditch we continue along the edge of the field with the stream on our left and without crossing the bridge ahead turn right following the main stream in trees.

Reaching the road we turn left and soon right up Dux Lane, passing several attractive houses and enjoying fine views on our left. We turn right at a T junction and at the next T junction cross to a stile in the hedge and continue ahead, later with the hedge on our left. At the road we turn right for a few yards then turn right on a track which soon goes downhill. After about ½ mile the track ends and we follow the fencing on our left into a strip of woods, cross a stream and are soon entering orchards. Here we turn right, keep straight ahead, go under pylon lines and at the boundary hedge cross a stile slightly to the right into a lane.

We turn right down the lane, cross a stream and turn left on a signposted footpath at first keeping the hedge on our left. As the hedge ends we bear right on a visible track, enjoying fine views. Near houses we continue forward on an enclosed path and reach the road at Basted, with The Plough on our left.

We turn left downhill and at the bottom turn right on a private road (which, in spite of the notice, is a public right of way for pedestrians) with a mill stream and the pleasantly landscaped industrial complex of Butterworths on our right. We pass a lake and as the road later bends left, we take a path on the right into trees, cross a stream and go uphill, later continuing over a drive and a residential road. Maintaining direction on The Landway, we reach the road and turn right into the centre of Borough Green, crossing the A25 and continuing up the High Street to the station car park.

REFRESHMENTS: Inns at Basted and Borough Green.

WALK 13

MAP: OS Landranger 188

SHIPBOURNE
⋧⋖

FAIRLAWNE PARK, PLAXTOL, IGHTHAM MOTE,
6 MILES

This is a varied walk suitable for any time of year, giving extensive views and a chance to see two noteworthy houses: Fairlawne, an early 18th-century house of Kentish ragstone with belfry and cupola, and Ightham Mote, a beautiful medieval moated manor house dating back to 1340, with important later additions. It is in the care of the National Trust and open to the public.

HOW TO GET THERE: Limited bus service between Borough Green and Tonbridge. By car on the A25 turning off at Ightham on the A227 for Shipbourne. There is ample car parking along Upper Green Road opposite Shipbourne church.

We continue along Upper Green Road and turn left with tennis courts on our left and gardens on our right, forking right to a stile. We turn right, soon turning left downhill. After crossing a bridge we continue forward across a meadow to a gate leading to a surfaced drive into Fairlawne Estate. We pass the mill pond on our left and soon another drive comes in from the right. We turn right to cross this and go uphill on a grassy path to a gate into Fairlawne Park. Continuing up the hill we pass three large trees on our left and make for a yellow waymarker post. At the post we turn right (ignoring other yellow posts which mark another footpath) along the bridlepath to a field gate in fencing and on towards the corner of the woods on our right. We then turn down the avenue of lime trees to the road.

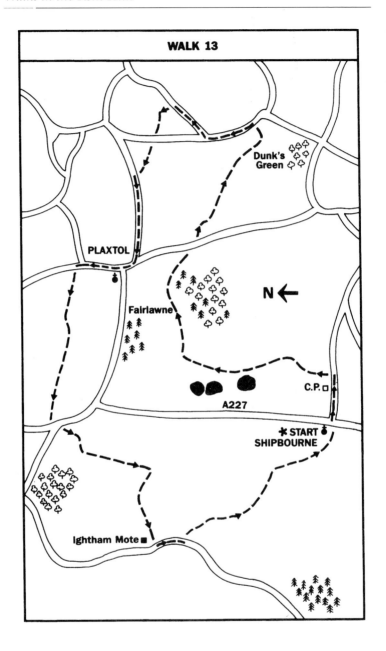

We turn right for a few yards, turn left over a stile, then bear right to a stile, taking us through a strip of woods to another stile where we turn left. We now follow the fence on our left and when this ends we maintain direction over a long field towards houses on the outskirts of Dunk's Green. We turn left over a stile and follow the path, finally bearing left to the road.

After turning left through Dunk's Green, we turn right down Allens Lane and at a bridge turn left over a stile. We follow the stream for a short distance then bear left to a gate and stile visible in the hedge. We cross the road diagonally right to a signposted footpath shortly continuing direction through the attractive village of Plaxtol. At a T junction we turn right past the picturesque 16th-century Plaxtol Forge, now a licensed restaurant. At the church it is well worth making a short diversion up Church Row to see a charming corner of Plaxtol, though the cottages are mostly no older than mid 19th century. The church itself dates from 1649 but was greatly enlarged and restored in the 19th century. It has a fine pair of elaborate brass chandeliers dated 1785.

We pass the church on our left and just beyond a right turning, we turn left on a signposted bridleway, between houses, soon going through orchards. We leave the orchards through a gap in the hedge to enter Fairlawne Estate and maintain direction going gently uphill. At a stile in a fence ahead we turn right on the bridleway with trees on our left, later entering woods. We continue to the road where we cross to a signposted bridleway opposite.

We soon ignore a left turning and bear right through woods; this section of the bridleway tends to be rather muddy in winter or wet weather. Emerging from the wood we continue direction down a field, keeping a line of fenced trees on our right and finally turning right through a gate into a hedged track. We follow this and eventually go downhill on a surfaced drive passing Ightham Mote on our right before bearing left through the entrance gates. Ightham Mote is open from April to October, except Tuesdays and Saturdays, 12 noon to 5.30 pm.

We continue down the road and after passing Mote Farm we turn left on a signposted footpath at first parallel with the road. After crossing a stile we have trees on our left until another stile takes us into woods. We follow a well-defined track and on leaving the woods we go downhill bearing left with trees over on our right. As the wood ends we turn right following Greensand Way waymarks to go through Shipbourne churchyard out to the road with Upper Green Road ahead.

Refreshments: General stores and post office in Dunks Green. Choice of inns at Plaxtol and inn at Shipbourne next to the church.

WALK 14

MAP: OS Landranger 188

HADLOW, WEST PECKHAM

6 MILES

This walk starts at the church in the village of Hadlow, with its history going back over a thousand years and its many historic buildings. It is particularly recommended for spring when the fruit trees are in blossom.

HOW TO GET THERE: By car on the A26.

Leaving the church of St Mary, Hadlow, we go along picturesque Church Street to the main road where we turn right and right again down Court Lane (public toilets on the corner) for about ⅓ mile. We turn left at a crossroads and just past a house on the right turn left over a stile, keeping forward between orchards to a gap in the hedge and turning right round the edge of the irregularly shaped field. At a corner with the cemetery hedge about 80 yards over on our right, instead of turning we maintain direction across a field with oast houses ahead on the left. We pass the end of a hedge on the right and in a few yards turn right and almost immediately left with a wire fence on our right. We follow this path to the main road where we turn right, soon passing The Harrow. After about 150 yards we turn left on a signposted footpath starting as a tarmac drive and soon continuing at the side of a house and garden, which we pass on our left.

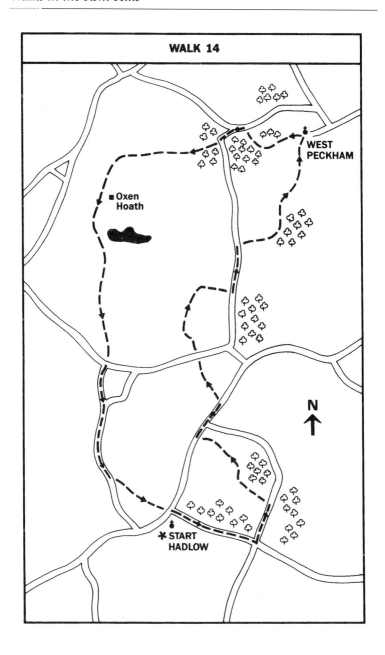

WALK 14

Oxen Hoath

WEST PECKHAM

N

✱ START
HADLOW

Reaching a road, we cross to a footpath opposite and shortly emerge in a sports field where we turn right round the edge, passing the end of the pavilion on our left. We bear left across a grassy track, turning right to a track with a hedge on our right and fence on our left. We are soon on a surfaced lane which we follow to the road where we turn left.

Just before a house on the right, we turn right over a stile, going forward along the edge of a field to cross a stile in the left hand corner of the field. We cross a stream and continue through trees then cross a stile into a field with fenced woods on our right. At a hut on the left our track turns right and when the track bears left leave it and continue ahead towards cottages and out onto a drive going through farm buildings. We turn right round an oast house into the tiny but charming village of West Peckham. The Swan is straight ahead across the village green and to the left of it is the ancient church of St Dunstan, dating from the 11th century and well worth visiting.

Turning right on leaving the church, we cross the green to a broken kissing gate and go forward on a track. On reaching a bungalow we turn right and go over a stile opposite the bungalow keeping a line of poplars on our right, turning left at the top of the field, ignoring a stile on our right then crossing a stile into an enclosed footpath. This emerges on the road just before a cottage on the right and after passing this we turn right on a signposted track for ½ mile. When the track turns left in a U bend we continue through an iron gate of the Oxenhoath Estate, shortly passing on our left the fine house which dates from late 18th century or early 19th century with a dome added in 1878. The nearby brick cottage dates from the 17th century and we pass ornamental gardens on our right.

We go through gateposts and leaving the track we continue ahead down a field then bear left towards two poplar trees, where we cross a stile beside a gate. As we go gently downhill on the grass track we have wide expansive views and a sight of the spectacular 170 ft high tower of Hadlow Castle, known as May's Folly, built by William Barton May in 1838-1840.

We reach the road by crossing a stile a few yards to the right of a gate and take the side turning straight ahead, thus maintaining direction. At the next road junction we bear right, later passing an inn on the right. After passing Twyford Road on the left we go through posts on the left to a tarmac path, following it to the main road through Hadlow village where Church Street is a few yards away to the left.

REFRESHMENTS: Hadlow where there is a choice of inns. The Swan at West Peckham.

WALK 15

MAP: OS Landranger 188

COWDEN
❧

7 MILES OR 9 MILES

This walk gives plenty of good open views and a chance to see two manor houses and some beautiful old buildings in the heart of Cowden village.

HOW TO GET THERE: By train to Hever station where there is also a car park.

From the upside platform of Hever station we take a rising footpath and soon turn right, doubling back at a higher level. After a gate we go slightly diagonally left to a waymarked post by trees then bear slightly left to another waymarked post visible after passing over the slight hill against trees ahead. We now go diagonally left to a pond in trees, and pass over two stiles. When the trees on our right end, we continue through farm buildings on a cart track then through a garden to the road where we turn left past Lydens Farm.

Just past a row of cottages we turn left on a signposted footpath crossing several stiles and following a field fence on our left to a small bridge. After crossing this we keep straight ahead, over a stile and then go diagonally right to a metal gate in the corner of the field. With Brook Street Farm on our left and a pleasant lake on our right, we pass through the garden of Oast Cottage to reach the road.

We cross the drive of Little Brook Street, later maintaining direction on a path on the right of the drive. After crossing a stile we continue between two hedges, cross another stile, and

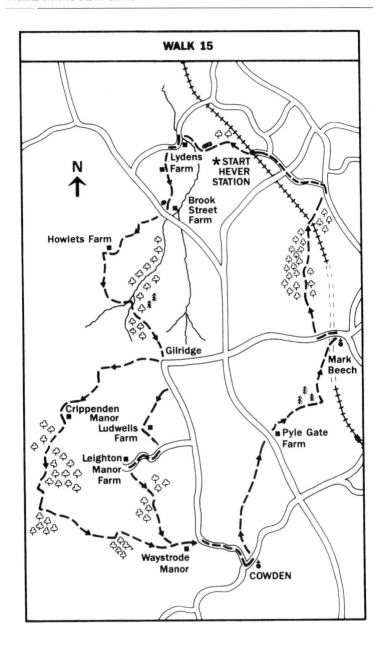

WALK 15

N

Lydens
Farm

★ START
HEVER
STATION

Brook
Street
Farm

Howlets Farm

Gilridge

Mark
Beech

Crippenden
Manor
Ludwells
Farm

Pyle Gate
Farm

Leighton
Manor
Farm

Waystrode
Manor

COWDEN

continue with the hedge on our left, then go over a stile on our left and continue with the hedge on our right. We soon pass a disused stile and bear left across the next field to a stile. We cross this and go forward on a gravel drive with Howlets Farm on our right. A stile takes us to the drive of Cobhambury Farm, the first part of which runs along the route of an old Roman road.

Leaving the drive immediately, by a farmhouse on our left, we cross a stile on the left and continue down a field with the hedge on our left. We pass a stile on the right without taking it and continue. Another stile takes us into woods and after crossing a stream we go forward for a short distance to a waymarked post where we take a path on the right doubling back at a higher level. After crossing a plank bridge on our right, we turn left uphill and follow the path through woods for over ¼ mile. We leave the woods by a stile and continue with a fence on our right to cross a stile to a drive where we turn right to the road.

FOR THE SHORTER VERSION: We maintain direction on the road opposite for about 150 yards. Just before a house on the right, we turn right at a gate on a signposted footpath, keeping the trees on our right. After crossing a stile we make for the next stile ahead and slightly left, continue diagonally left to cross a stile near a large oak tree, maintain direction over another stile and then a gap in the hedge and finally reach a farm. Having crossed a stile into the farm area, we turn left on a surfaced drive.

At a T junction we turn right on a track, soon ignoring a stile on the left. We pass a left turning and go downhill to a bridge. Without crossing it, we turn left and follow the fence on our left with Leighton Manor Farm on our right. Opposite this beautiful complex of buildings we turn left through a gate then continue through the field with a fence on our right. Shortly we cross a stile beside a gate and enter woods on a small path which at once turns right. We follow this twisting path for ½ mile, later with a drop on our right and eventually at a gate emerge on the drive of Waystrode Manor.

FOR THE LONGER VERSION: On our right is the private road to Crippenden Manor. We follow this for over ½ mile not taking the path on the left or the first two paths on the right, the road finally bearing left between farm buildings. Opposite the manor house, a picturesque tile-hung building which dates from 1607, we turn right across a lawn with a pond on our right. We bear left and continue with the fence on our right until we pass through a gap in it. Almost immediately we pass through a gate in another fence and cross a field, maintaining direction, to a path through a strip of woods leading to a large field. Here we turn left and follow a path round the edge with trees on our left and a fence on our right. This path turns right and then left round the corners of the field. Where the field ends we bear left then immediately turn left across a stile to a small path into trees, soon passing a pond on our right and crossing a stile to a field.

We follow the hedge on the right round two sides of the field, eventually reaching a stile by a gate which we cross and continue downhill with the hedge on our left. Soon we cross a stile on the left, maintain direction with the hedge on our right, cross a stile on our right then continue on a cart track. About 100 yards beyond a derelict barn on our left, at the end of the field we turn left on a track into woods. Soon we turn right and go diagonally right down a field with woods over on our right. A gap in the hedge brings us to the next field where we bear slightly left to a well-defined path which takes us down to an iron bridge. We cross this and follow the path through woods, turn right on a crossing path and eventually emerge through a gate on the drive of Waystrode Manor.

BOTH VERSIONS NOW CONTINUE TOGETHER: Passing a lake, on our right we have a good view of this impressive timber-framed and gabled manor house, parts of which date back to the 13th and 14th centuries. On reaching the road we go right maintaining direction and are shortly in the village of Cowden with its many beautiful old buildings. At a T junction in the centre of the village we turn left passing the church, parts of which date back to the 13th century. The shingled spire dates from the early 14th century and is considerably out of perpendicular. In the 17th century Cowden was a prosperous centre of the Wealden ironworking industry and in the church and churchyard some of the memorials are slabs of cast iron dating from the 17th and 18th centuries.

Just past the church we turn left on a signposted footpath and follow the fence on our left, then cross the field, maintaining direction. We cross two successive stiles in front of a bungalow and go forward on a footpath. Later, at a left turning into woods, we fork right downhill with the hedge on our right. After crossing a stream by a bridge with a stile we go uphill making for a barn, the roof of which is clearly visible. At the top of the hill, in the fence to the left, we cross a stile and continue towards barns where another stile takes us through a farm area to the road.

We cross to the Pyle Gate Farm entrance opposite, then bear left on a track which soon turns right. We follow this descending, wooded track, ignoring paths to the left, for about ½ mile, when we turn left to another track at a T junction, past a tree on a central 'island'.

(At this point it would be possible to shorten the walk by turning *right* on the crossing track for ½ mile to Cowden station, the next station after Hever. The last part of the track is parallel with the railway line and on reaching the road the station approach is on the left.)

Soon after passing a quaint little cottage on the left, we turn right out of the woods, cross a stile and go up the side of a field with the hedge on our left. After crossing a stile on our left, we cross a small field, cross a stile on the other side, and continue with woods on our right at the end of which we bear right into another field making for Markbeech church. We pass through a bar gate into the churchyard and turn left to the road where we turn left for about 200 yards.

Beside the entrance to Bramsell's Farm we turn right on a

fenced footpath and follow it for about 1 mile, the middle
section going through woods. After emerging from this we
maintain direction, later bearing right under the railway and
finally out to the road. We turn left and shortly left again on a
side turning. We later continue over crossroads and turn left up
to a road where we turn left for about 200 yards.

REFRESHMENTS: Cowden and Markbeech.

MAP: OS Landranger 188

COWDEN, HILL HOATH, CHIDDINGSTONE HOATH

8 MILES

This walk gives us some splendid views, together with the sight of interesting and ancient houses, several skilfully restored. From time to time there are outcrops of huge sandstone rocks which are characteristic of this part of Kent.

HOW TO GET THERE: By train to Cowden station where there is also a car park. By car on the B2026.

From Cowden station approach we fork left to the road where we turn left uphill to take the first turning on the right. We follow this lane for about ⅓ mile when we turn left on a signposted track, soon through a gate and over a stile on the right and continuing over a field with some cottages away on our left. After crossing a stile in the hedge we maintain direction, ie straight ahead towards a 'finger' of woods ahead, passing it on our right and entering the wood by a stile in the corner. We go down a fairly steep path to cross a footbridge, up the other side and turn left on a path at the edge of the wood. This later ends with a kissing gate and we then bear diagonally right up to a footpath sign where we turn left on a cart track to the road.

We turn right on the road, ignoring a left fork, and soon pass Hoath House, a picturesque half-timbered 16th-century building with a number of later additions and alterations. A ¼

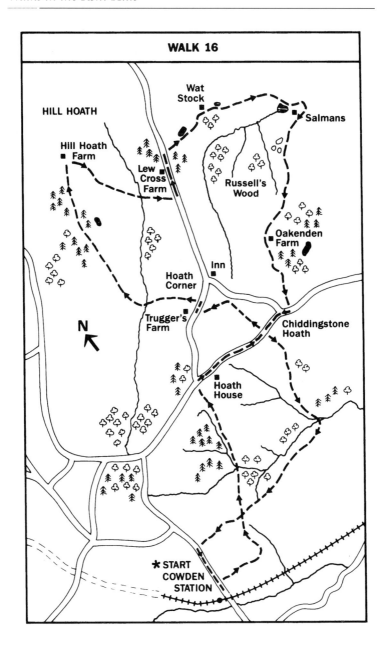

mile further on we turn left at a signpost and stile on a rising footpath through shrubbery and over a stile on our left into a field where the path follows the line of overhead wires. At a crossing path before trees, we turn left, following wires, to cross a stile in the hedge. We continue diagonally downhill making for farm buildings visible ahead. Crossing a stile to the road we turn right and soon left (if refreshment is required, The Rock at Hoath Corner is about 200 yards further along the road). The signposted footpath takes us downhill with a hedge on the right and we follow it, bearing right, down through woodland and up to a field where we turn right and on to a young woodland. We emerge on a main track and turn right; shortly ignoring a path on the right we keep left and the path merges into a wide fenced path. We cross a stile on the right then turn left on a waymarked field path to a stile soon reaching the hamlet of Hill Hoath. Just past an attractive timbered house on the left, we turn right through a farm area. We ignore a path on the left and soon continue on a fenced track which continues as a wide field path. After passing an attractive man-made pond we bear right to a line of trees then bear left, keeping right of the trees to a stile in the corner which we cross. We turn left then right on a well-defined path through woodland bearing left over a stream to a stile on the left just before two gates and make our way up the side of a field with sundry trees on our right.

Reaching the road we turn left and after ¼ mile turn right on the drive of Wat Stock Farm and later right opposite the first barn. Our track later becomes a surfaced drive and we pass a lake and some beautiful residences incorporating former oast houses. The drive turns left but we maintain direction and then turn right over a drive and up to a rather hidden footpath with the picturesque house Salmans, dating from the late 17th century, on our right. There are footpath diversions round the house – please follow new waymarks. After ¼ mile we cross a stile on our left and continue direction with a fence on our right. We cross a stile in the field corner maintaining direction to another stile and go on to join a track diagonally right to continue through a small plantation after which we go up a sloping field with the hedgerow on our right. At the top of the field we cross a stile and turn left on a path which soon becomes a lane.

After passing one or two interesting houses we eventually reach the road and turn right into Chiddingstone Hoath, a hamlet built round a road junction. We turn left on the road signposted to Cowden and Edenbridge and soon turn left over a stile opposite the one we crossed earlier in the walk. Keeping the hedge on our left we go down to the end of the field and after passing a gate and stile on the left bear slightly right to cross a stile. We continue ahead to a stile on the right just before a barrier to go diagonally left downhill with a fence on the left. We bear left to a stile taking us into woods and go forward on a well-defined path down to a footbridge, continuing on a diagonal path on the right.

The right of way is along the left side of this elongated field and after noticing some large outcrops of rock in trees on our left, we eventually come to a stile taking us into a chestnut plantation. On leaving this we maintain direction uphill and at the top we go on to a cattle trough near a stile in the hedge ahead (this is one we crossed early in the walk). Once over the stile we turn right with the hedge and later a fence on our right and finally cross a stile into a small wood with a pond on the right. Emerging from the wood we continue direction over a field then bear left with the hedge on our right down to a stile and the road. Here we turn left and later right on the station approach road.

REFRESHMENTS: The Rock at Hoath Corner.

MAP: OS Landranger 188

KENT WATER,
RIVER MEDWAY
❧

9 MILES; OMITTING THE MEDWAY, 7¾ MILES

This walk includes the sight of beautiful old houses, pleasant aspects, riverside paths and some interesting rock formations.

HOW TO GET THERE: By train to Cowden station, where there is also a car park.

From the station approach we turn left up the road and shortly right on a signposted lane, following it for about ½ mile. Just past Wickens Farm we fork right and cross a rather obscure stile into a sloping field, cross it diagonally left up to a telegraph pole and continue forward with trees on our left. Soon we turn right on a cart track with a hedge on our left and go down through a gate and farm area to the road where we turn right for ¼ mile. Just before a house we turn left over a stile keeping the fence on our right as we make for a bridge in trees ahead.

We cross the bridge over a stream known as Kent Water (it forms part of the boundary between Kent and East Sussex), go over a stile on the left and follow the stream in trees on our left over two more stiles; the last one is slightly to the right of the field corner. We shortly turn left under the railway then turn diagonally right along the field gradually getting nearer to the trees on our left. Ignoring a gated bridge on our left we go over a stile keeping forward to another bridge ahead. We cross this

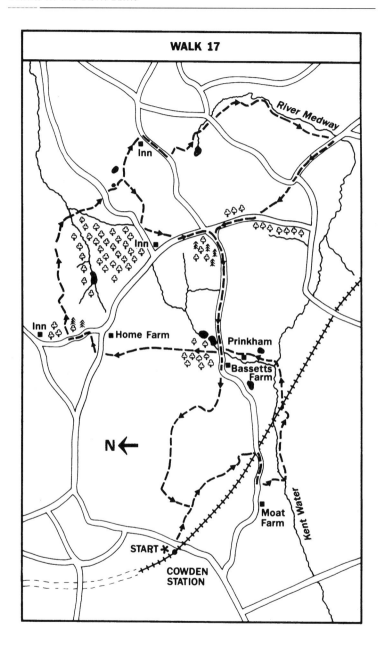

bridge and make for a stile at the far end of a field, cross it and keep along the edge of the field to another stile, then pass on our left a barn and an attractive old timber-framed house, Prinkham.

Having followed the drive to a minor road we turn left for a few yards then right on a signposted footpath up to a gate. We go forward uphill, cross two fields by stiles in fencing and as the next field ends bear right to cross a stile beside a gate resuming direction up the field with the fence on the left. We finally cross a stile on the left, keep the hedge on our right, cross a stile in the field corner and continue direction to the road.

We take a footpath opposite, shortly ignore a stile on the left and finally bear left on a drive to a road where we turn left and soon right over a stile. (If needed there is an inn a short distance along the road.) This track gives good views on the left before it later goes downhill past some large rocks and down the side of a field. When the fencing on the left ends, we go over a stile and bear right following a hedge to a stile and a lane where we turn left. After another stile we go down a field with the hedgerow on our left, pass a pond on the right, cross a stile and continue through a small plantation. We soon turn right on a shingle track; when it turns left we maintain direction on a path. Later, in trees, we turn left across a bridge and continue with a vineyard on the left and fenced woods on the right. We turn right at the corner of the woods, pass a pond on the left, cross a 'double' bridge then continue forward slightly right to a bridge in the hedgerow. From here we continue uphill slightly right, through a few trees, then maintain direction to a stile in trees ahead. A fairly steep path takes us up to the road, where we cross to a stepped path opposite. We bear left over a field to a pond hidden in trees and go forward.

FOR THE SHORTER VERSION: With a house over on our left, we turn right across a large field making for the right hand corner of a small wood ahead. We go through a gap in the hedge and bear right to the far right hand corner of the field. On reaching the road, without going into it we turn left over a stile keeping a fence and soon woods on our left. We maintain direction down the field to a stile and a road, where we turn left. (There is an inn to the right along the road.) At a crossroads we turn right on the road signposted to Bassetts and Cowden.

FOR THE LONGER VERSION: With a house over on our left we go forward to follow fencing and shortly before reaching a trig point we turn left over a stile. We bear right to a stile in the corner of the field finally turning right on a drive to the road.

We turn right passing The Bottle House Inn and a pleasant row of weather-boarded cottages. After about ¼ mile we turn left on a signposted footpath which begins as a surfaced drive and later bends right. Shortly we turn left uphill to a gate and signposted footpath and go forward initially with garden fencing over on our right. We maintain direction with trees and a steep drop on our right. At the end of the trees we turn right downhill making for a bridge over a stream; the path here is decidedly boggy, particularly in winter. After crossing the bridge we bear left following the stream to a stile and the road.

We cross to a stile opposite, passing one or two freestanding trees on our right as we make for a bridge directly ahead by a willow. Once over the stream we bear right making for the left hand end of a distant line of trees. The river Medway is over on our left; we touch it at a bend as we go forward towards the trees and again as we reach the trees where we cross a stile. For nearly ½ mile we now follow the river bank, passing two weirs and crossing a bar stile near the second one. Reaching the road at Chafford Bridge we turn right for about ⅓ mile. Soon after a left turning the road turns sharply right but we maintain direction by crossing a stile slightly to the left and going up a field with the hedge on our left. We continue over a stile enjoying good views as we look back and finally reach the road through a gate on our left. Maintaining direction to a crossroads, we turn left on the road signposted to Bassetts and Cowden.

BOTH VERSIONS NOW CONTINUE TOGETHER: We follow this pleasant minor road for nearly ¾ mile, passing one or two beautiful 16th and 17th-century houses. After passing Bassetts, a fine timbered house (not to be confused with Bassetts Mill already passed), the road goes uphill and bends left, but we turn right through a gate and along the edge of a field with trees and large rocks on our left. At the field corner we continue on a track which soon bears right. We go through a gate and forward with the hedge on our left. After bearing left beside woods, at the top of the hill we bear right diagonally down to the far corner of the field. At a point about 30 yards to the left of the corner, a downhill cart track takes us through woods to a gate and open fields. With rocks and trees on our left, we continue to a stile and a path through a chestnut plantation.

Leaving the plantation we continue direction to the post at the top of the hill then bear right past a cattle trough down to a stile in the hedge near cottages. After crossing a stile we go forward with cottages over on our right, cross another stile and turn left to go down a cart track to a lane. We turn right for ⅓ mile and left on the road to the station approach.

REFRESHMENTS: The Bottle House Inn and there are two other inns only a short distance off the route.

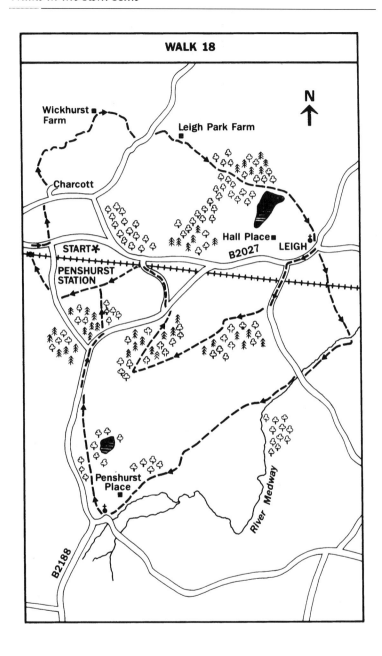

MAP: OS Landranger 188

LEIGH
❧

PENSHURST, PENSHURST PLACE, 7½ MILES
PENSHURST PARK, 5 MILES

This is a beautiful parkland and farmland walk with fine expansive views and only the gentlest of gradients.

HOW TO GET THERE: By train or bus to Penshurst station. By car on the B2027. Access to the car park is down the road on the east side of the station then turning right towards the railway line.

Leaving Penshurst station on the north side, we turn right up the B2027 road soon passing St Luke's church on the right and immediately turning left on an enclosed footpath over fields. Coming out to a road, we turn right for a short distance then left on a small road (which bears right to the hamlet of Charcott and The Greyhound Inn). We continue direction on a lane taking us towards farm buildings. Before the buildings we turn right over a signposted stile bearing left with the farm buildings on our left. A stile beside a gate takes us into the next field where we turn right keeping the hedge on our right for some distance until we reach a bridge on the right taking us over a stream. We continue forward with the hedge still on our right and go through a gap into the next field. From here the path lies diagonally uphill towards Wickhurst Farm. After passing a converted barn on our right, we turn right on a lane passing the farmhouse and an attractive double-oast residence.

We continue down the lane for about ¼ mile, reach the road

which we cross to a plank bridge over a stream, and turn left with the hedge on our left. As the field ends we go through a gate and turn right on a lane leading to Leigh Park Farm. Just past a pond and some oast houses we turn right into a field, keeping the hedge on our left until a stile takes us into woods. Later a fenced path takes us along the edge of the grounds of Hall Place. (This path is liable to be somewhat overgrown in high summer.) The path ends at a kissing gate where we turn right in a field with a fence on our right, soon passing the house, a Tudor-style mansion built in 1871-2. After another field, we come out to the road between a lodge and gatehouse of Hall Place. Here we may make an optional diversion by turning right through the churchyard to visit the church. Some parts of St Mary's church, Leigh, date back to the 13th century but most of the present walls were rebuilt and the tower completed in the middle of the 19th century.

Turning right down the road, we are soon at the picturesque village of Leigh with its large village green, shop, toilets and several inns.

FOR THE LONGER VERSION: We cross the village green going down Green View Avenue and through a gate into a hedged track which takes us under a railway bridge. Continuing direction on an enclosed track, we then keep the hedge on our right and cross the next field making for a bridge ahead in trees. After crossing the river Medway, we turn left for about 20 yards then right over another bridge and keep right for a few yards to a squeeze stile. We turn right to a nearby plank bridge and another squeeze stile and continue forward for about ⅓ mile with the river hidden in trees on our right. On reaching the road we turn right over the Medway and immediately left over a stile.

We follow the river on our left, later bearing right to a bridge over a tributary. Once over the bridge we bear slightly left uphill passing on our left Killick's Bank, a pleasant house and cottage. Our path is now a surfaced farm track which we follow uphill.

Finally as the track bears left, we continue forward through a squeeze stile and go downhill, bearing slightly left and making for a large freestanding tree, beyond which we cross a stile. We go forward for a short distance along the edge of the field then bear left over a stile into a surfaced lane where we turn right.

We continue on this lane for over ½ mile, soon sighting ahead Penshurst Place, a fine 14th-century manor house with some 16th and early 19th-century alterations. (The house is open to the public every afternoon from April to September, except Monday, but open on Bank Holiday Mondays.)

Coming out under an arched gate to the road, we go forward for a few yards before turning right up some steps into the picturesque courtyard leading into the churchyard of Penshurst church. Before doing this we can make an optional diversion into the village of Penshurst where there are shops for teas and ices, an inn and toilets.

The exterior of the church is largely 19th-century, but parts of the interior date back to the 13th and 14th centuries. Continuing through the churchyard past the church, we go through a squeeze stile into Penshurst Park, passing Penshurst Place on our right and crossing the drive through squeeze stiles. As we keep forward the lake comes into sight on our right and, after crossing a stile in fencing, we go gradually uphill towards woods ahead. At the corner of the woods we maintain direction with the woods on our left. At the top of the hill we turn left over a stile and soon reach the road where we turn right. We are shortly at a road junction where we continue for 150 yards on the road signposted to Leigh then turn left on a signposted footpath into forestry plantations. Going downhill and over a crossing track we avoid side turnings and watch out for yellow waymarks on trees denoting the direction of the path. After crossing a stile and stream we turn left with a hopfield on our right, shortly coming out through the buildings of Moorden Farm to the road. We turn right and at the fork take the lane on the left back to the car park at the station.

FOR THE SHORTER VERSION: Going through the village of Leigh, we take the first turning on the left, signposted to Bidborough, soon going under the railway bridge at Leigh Halt and uphill past oasthouses. When the road flattens at a house named Pauls Hill, we turn right on a signposted footpath taking us into Penshurst Place Estate. We follow the track for about 1 mile passing a small pond on the right, bearing slightly left over a stile and continuing along a wide avenue of plane trees. Later we go through a squeeze stile, still continuing direction.

Immediately the avenue of trees ends we turn right and right again thus doubling back somewhat. Our path goes slightly downhill, crosses a stream bed, then goes uphill between plantations. When these end we go through the remains of a gate and turn left down to the road.

A few yards to the left we turn right down a pleasant lane for about ¼ mile. On our right we pass a railway bridge and soon cross a stile on the right, keeping along the side of a field with the hedgerow on our left. Later we continue with a hopfield on our right and woods on our left, coming out through the buildings of Moorden Farm to the road. We turn right and at a fork take the lane on the left back to the car park at the station.

REFRESHMENTS: Inns and shops at Leigh and Penshurst. Inn opposite Penshurst station. Inn at Charcott.

MAP: OS Landranger 188

SPELDHURST, BIDBOROUGH
❧

7½ MILES; OMITTING BIDBOROUGH, 5 MILES

These two attractive villages are situated on neighbouring ridges. Exploring the vicinity and enjoying the pleasant views inevitably involves a number of uphill and downhill stretches but the gradients are gentle.

HOW TO GET THERE: The walk starts from the village hall in St Mary's Lane, Speldhurst, where there is a car park. By car on the B2176 turning south for Speldhurst. Turn right into Northfields Road (the second on the right). St Mary's Lane turns right off Northfields Road.

We return to Northfields Road, turn right and soon turn left on the Penshurst road for about 50 yards to a signposted footpath on the right. This shortly continues between open fields then becomes enclosed as we go down to a minor road.

Here we turn right past a beautiful 15th-century house and left beside Old Bullingstone, keeping right at a fork and soon crossing a footbridge. Our path goes gradually uphill then flattens and after a stile we cross a field diagonally to a stile in fencing with a house over on our right. We maintain direction to another stile, pass a lake in trees on our right and reach the road where we cross to the turning opposite. As the road bends left, we turn right through a gate and in a few yards turn

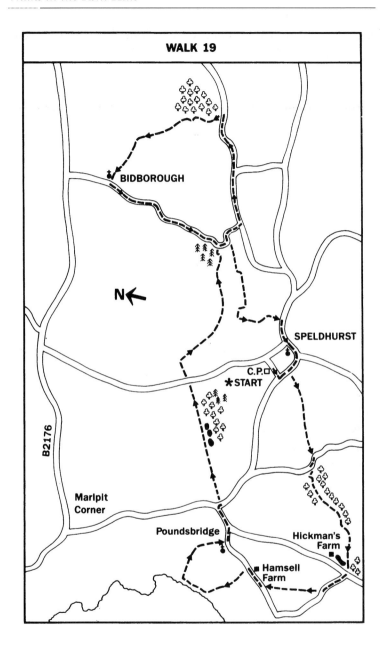

WALK 19

BIDBOROUGH

N

SPELDHURST

C.P.
★START

B2176

Marlpit
Corner

Poundsbridge

Hickman's
Farm

Hamsell
Farm

diagonally left down the field. We continue through a broken gate, cross a stile in the hedge and maintain direction over the next field to a stile in the hedge about 50 yards to the left of farm buildings.

Turning right on the road, we pass Hamsell Farm and turn left on a signposted footpath which soon brings us out over a stile into a field. We bear right round the edge and soon have the river Medway on our left, cross a stile into the next field and follow the river to a footbridge where we turn right, away from the Medway, with a ditch on our left. After going through a gate we bear right on a track up to the far left hand corner of the field, go through another gate and continue to the road with the churchyard of Poundsbridge church on our right. (There is a seat with a good view if a rest seems desirable.)

We turn left on the road and soon left at a T junction. At the next T junction we turn right round a half-timbered house bearing the date 1593. In a few yards we turn left over a stile into a field where we go forward with the hedgerow on our right. This footpath continues for nearly ¾ mile with pleasant views on the left, taking us past two ponds on the right and over various stiles as we go from one field to the next, until a final stretch of fenced path takes us to the road at the northern outskirts of Speldhurst.

A few yards to our left we take a signposted footpath on our right passing a house on our left. We are now on a surfaced track, which soon turns right with a stream on our left. Later we cross a bridge and continue uphill to a farm area, cross a step stile beside a gate and go forward to cross another stile on the left past a footpath sign on a large tree. We continue to another stile then diverge slightly to the left where a third stile brings us to the road where we turn right.

FOR THE LONGER VERSION TO BIDBOROUGH: We turn right for about ¼ mile to a T junction where we turn left, later ignoring a right turning. We go downhill and opposite the Pump House on the right, we turn left across the adjacent cemetery drive to a signposted uphill path passing some cottages and houses. Just past these we turn left on a footpath, shortly fork left downhill and over a stile, continue direction between fields and soon go uphill and through a patch of woods.

Emerging over a stile we continue with the cemetery on our left, cross a stile in wire fencing and follow the path into woods. We come out to a field, go downhill with the fencing on our left, cross a plank bridge, continue uphill, over a stile and up a road with houses on the left. Bearing left past the school we are soon at the entrance to St Lawrence's church, Bidborough, sited on a narrow spur of high ground giving fine views. It is Norman in origin with subsequent additions and restorations. We turn left down the minor road for nearly ¾ mile and pass the stile we recently crossed.

BOTH VERSIONS NOW CONTINUE TOGETHER: Just past the lodge of Scriventon, we turn right up steps, cross a stile slightly right to keep the hedge on our right. After two more stiles we reach a lane where we turn left for a few yards then right on a footpath through trees. We cross a footbridge, come out to a field, turn right and keep the trees on our right as we continue round the field edge to a stile. Here we turn left on a concrete drive, leaving it when it turns right and crossing a stile on the left. We bear right with the hedge on our right, cross another stile and continue to the road.

Turning right uphill into Speldhurst, we notice large rock outcrops on the left and pass St Mary's church on the right. This is well worth a visit. There are remains of the earlier 14th-century building though the present structure dates from 1870 and is notable for its stained glass windows designed by Burne-Jones. We continue on the Penshurst road for about 150 yards and turn right down Northfields Road back to the village hall.

REFRESHMENTS: Inns at Speldhurst. The Hare and Hounds at Bidborough.

··········
WALK 20
··········

MAP: OS Landranger 188

ASHURST, GROOMBRIDGE
❧

7¾ MILES

*With only a few moderate uphill paths we can enjoy parkland,
several beautiful old houses and wide sweeping views across the
Weald. The walk is suitable for any time of year though some
paths will be muddy in winter. In early spring Ashurst church
surrounded by snowdrops makes a pleasant picture.*

HOW TO GET THERE: By train to Ashurst station. By car on the
A264.

We turn left down the station approach and just before the road
we turn right over a stile, go uphill to the left hand corner of the
field, over a stile and forward to the road where we turn right to
St Martin's church. The original building was 10th century but
the present one dates from the second half of the 19th century.
It has a Norman font and one of the bells in the attractive
wooden belfry is dated 1612.

Turning right through the churchyard, or on the lane beside
it, we turn right again on a signposted footpath starting on a
drive. When this bends right, we turn left on a field path,
continuing with a hedge and later a wooded hollow on our left.
At the end of the woods we bear left at a concrete drive and take
a signposted footpath across a field to a gate and stile. We
continue downhill over a crossing path marked W.W. to a stile

93

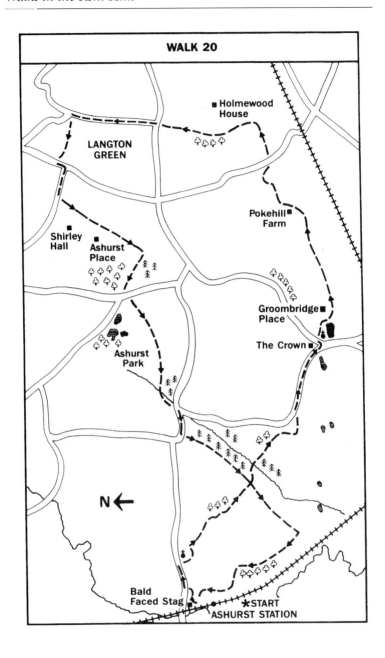

into woods. We follow this well-defined path downhill, over a stream and uphill. Soon we bear left along a tree-fringed track which terminates in double metal gates. We turn right on an estate road shortly reaching steps either side, when we turn left up to a stile and go forward over the field to a stile and road where we turn right.

We are soon on the outskirts of Groombridge, a village with many lovely old buildings. On reaching the village green we bear left past a row of picturesque 18th-century brick and tile-hung cottages.

Opposite the 16th-century Crown Inn we take a footpath and cross a field with the Groombridge Place lake on our right. We go through a gate, following waymarks and continuing past Groombridge Place, shortly turning left with a good view of the house. This fine 17th-century house of mellowed brick, sometimes visited by the diarist John Evelyn, stands on the square moated site of an earlier medieval house. We follow fencing on our left past the house, continue to a kissing gate then follow a well-defined path over meadows with the stream nearby on our right. Maintaining direction over two more stiles and a bridge, we then keep a ditch and later a fence on our left till at a farm we cross another stile and drive to a grass path. We shortly turn right on a wide, hedged path and follow it to a stile and a road.

Crossing to the track opposite, we later go through a gate and forward to cross a bridge and turn left up a bridleway. On reaching a road we continue direction uphill. At the main road (A264) we cross to Farnham Lane, following it for ½ mile. Opposite a right turning, we turn left over a waymarked stile then go downhill to a stile and footbridge over a stream. We go diagonally left up a field to trees, continuing with a hedgerow on our right and shortly bearing right through a gap to a post in front of trees ahead. We soon bear right over grass to a stile and the road where we turn left.

We shortly turn right on the Fordcombe road and just before Danemore Farm drive on the right we turn left on a signposted footpath, going diagonally right then crossing a stile and maintaining direction. We cross a stile to a drive and a second stile then go forward to a double stile in the right hand corner of the field and follow a visible field path with playing fields on our left and Ashurst Place on our right. At a fence we cross a stile and continue ahead through a squeeze gate and across a field to a double stile, taking the left hand one, shortly turning right on a fenced path to a stile. When the path ends we continue direction towards a house and kissing gate to reach the road.

Crossing to a drive opposite (this looks private but is a public footpath) we soon continue on a track and maintain direction, keeping a fence on our right and enjoying a good view of Ashurst Park House, a handsome early Victorian mansion. Still following the fence on our right, we finally cross a somewhat hidden bridge in the field corner before bearing left on a path to the road where we turn right for about 200 yards.

At the bend in the road we turn left on a signposted footpath beside the entrance to Stone Cross House. When this ends we continue forward with a fence up on our right and cross a stile beside a gate. We go forward on a visible path round the hillside enjoying good views ahead, later continuing over a stile beside a gate and maintaining direction. After crossing the left hand stile we continue down to another stile on our right and turn left on a path, later turning right. We maintain direction for ½ mile before turning left on a downhill lane and right just before a house. We pass a splendid old house and soon reach Ashurst station forecourt.

REFRESHMENTS: The Bald-faced Stag inn in Ashurst and inns in Groombridge.